Advance Praise for **Personality Isn't Permanent**

"This is a generous, empowering and purposeful book. If you're ready, it will help you unlock a future that you may have been brainwashed into believing wasn't possible. Worth sharing a copy with someone you care about."

—Seth Godin, author of *This Is Marketing*

"*Personality Isn't Permanent* is possibly the best self-help book I've ever read, and a book that will redefine the genre. After this book, it's no longer good enough to talk about untested theory—Ben backs everything up with both amazing stories and cutting edge, tested science, while still making it actionable to anyone. Best part: this is the book that destroys all the useless personality test peddlers that infect the world."

—Tucker Max, *New York Times* bestselling author

"In *Personality Isn't Permanent*, Dr. Hardy crushes an outdated paradigm and gives you the process to create a bigger, bolder future."

—JJ Virgin, *New York Times* bestselling author

"Ben Hardy is proof of what he writes about. He keeps getting better and better—and so can you."

—Ryan Holiday, bestselling author of *Stillness Is the Key*

"For those looking to up their game, *Personality Isn't Permanent* is more than a hopeful and fascinating read, it is utterly applicable. In the crowded space of self-help/business, Benjamin Hardy's book is a game changer."

—Richard Paul Evans, *New York Times* bestselling author

"*Personality Isn't Permanent* beautifully illustrates why people get stuck and provides a science-based process to help you transform yourself and your life. This is required reading for anyone who wants to improve their self-awareness and success!"

—Dr. Tasha Eurich, *New York Times* bestselling
author of *Insight* and *Bankable Leadership*

"*Personality Isn't Permanent* is a supremely brilliant work and a must read. Addressing trauma and addiction in a hopeful and impactful way. You can rewrite your story."

—Glenn Morshower, award-winning actor, producer, and director

"Dr. Hardy enlightens you on the role trauma plays in shaping your personality. Change is possible when past traumas are healed. Personality is in a continual state of change. This book will help you write your future story."

—Dr. Donald Wood, founder and CEO of Inspired Performance Institute

Personality
Isn't Permanent

Personality Isn't Permanent

Break Free from Self-Limiting Beliefs
and Rewrite Your Story

Benjamin Hardy, PhD

PORTFOLIO / PENGUIN

PORTFOLIO / PENGUIN
An imprint of Penguin Random House LLC
penguinrandomhouse.com

Most Portfolio books are available at a discount when purchased in quantity for sales promotions or corporate use.
Special editions, which include personalized covers, excerpts,
and corporate imprints, can be created when purchased in
large quantities. For more information, please call (212) 572-
2232 or e-mail specialmarkets@penguinrandomhouse.com.
Your local bookstore can also assist with discounted bulk pur-
chases using the Penguin Random House corporate Business-
to-Business program. For assistance in locating a participating
retailer, e-mail B2B@penguinrandomhouse.com.

Library of Congress Cataloging-in-Publication Data

Names: Hardy, Benjamin, author.
Title: Personality isn't permanent : break free from
    self-limiting beliefs and rewrite your story /
    Benjamin Hardy.
Description: New York : Portfolio, 2020. | Includes
    bibliographical references and index.
Identifiers: LCCN 2020002302 (print) |
    LCCN 2020002303 (ebook) |
    ISBN 9780593083314 (hardcover) |
    ISBN 9780593083321 (ebook)
Subjects: LCSH: Personality. | Motivation (Psychology) |
    Self-actualization (Psychology)
Classification: LCC BF698 .H337 2020 (print) |
    LCC BF698 (ebook) | DDC 155.2—dc23
LC record available at https://lccn.loc.gov/2020002302
LC ebook record available at https://lccn.loc.gov/2020002303

ISBN 9780593328965 (international edition)

Printed in the United States of America
10 9 8 7 6 5 4 3 2

BOOK DESIGN BY NICOLE LAROCHE

For Lauren.

*Thank you for betting on me when it made
no sense and for continuing to bet on me.*

It still doesn't make much sense.

I love you forever.

May our future always be brighter than our past.

Contents

Conclusion

A painting is never finished—it simply stops in interesting places.

—*Paul Gardner*

Personality
Isn't Permanent

A Personality Test Almost Ruined My Life

My wife—the woman I love the most in the world and have five wonderful children with—almost didn't marry me . . . *because of a personality test.*

A very popular personality test while I was in college was called the Color Code, which categorizes people into one of four colors. Reds are your type A go-getters, driven by ambition and self-interest. Blues are heart-centered and relationship-based. Whites are introspective and often passive. Yellows seek fun and are the life of the party.

Lauren was a Red. So when her family found out that I was a White, they were very concerned. Lauren had previously been married to an abusive and self-absorbed guy, who was also a Red. Her parents thought, given her interest in me, that she might be going too far in the opposite direction to compensate. Or that she was being overly cautious to avoid the trauma of her prior marriage.

Like many others who put stock in personality tests, Lauren's family considered the Color Code to have some validity and truth. They saw people through the test's lens—as one of four types.

"If this guy is a White, and she's a Red, she's going to walk all over him," were their genuine concerns. "She needs a real man, not a White."

She was wondering the same thing. Could a Red and a White really work together? Whites rarely get promoted at work. Whites are pushovers. Whites are dreamers but don't stick to long-term goals.

Luckily for me, Lauren gave me a chance. She got to know me, and after we were together awhile in a great relationship, she took the leap of faith against her prejudgment of Whites and her parents' initial concerns.

Lauren and I laugh about this now, happily married with five kids and fourteen years of combined formal psychology education later. But the fact remains: *A personality test almost ruined our life together.*

I'm not the only one who's been misdiagnosed or unfairly limited by a personality test. In fact, you likely have also fallen prey to this epidemic. The Color Code is just one of countless popular "personality" frameworks sweeping through modern culture. Some other major culprits include the Myers-Briggs Type Indicator, the DISC assessment, the Winslow Personality Test, NEO, HEXACO, Birkman, Enneagram, inkblots, and more.

The list goes on and it doesn't stop. It won't stop. It seems like hundreds of new tests are devised every single day.

The obsession with "personality" is so ridiculous that in 2019 Facebook had to ban personality quizzes and other apps with "minimal utility." This happened after more than 87 million people had given away their personal information in exchange for the answer to a personality quiz.

Personality tests can be interesting, entertaining, and playful, yes. But there's a dark reality about them, and the entire notion of "personality" in general, which limits—and in some cases *ruins*—the lives of countless people.

The mainstream perspective is that your personality is the real and authentic you. Your personality is "innate" and, for the most part, *unchangeable*. As a result, your job as a human being is to gather enough information and experience—to find the right personality test—in order to adequately "discover" your "hidden" personality.

Once you make this all-important discovery, you are then enabled to build your entire life around that personality. This life you build may not be the one you'd have chosen for yourself, but it's the life you were born to live. It's the hand you were dealt. To do anything otherwise would be disastrous, painful, and delusional.

Through all of this is the underlying assumption that *you were born "hardwired" as the person you are, and you cannot change that.*

The truth is, though, that virtually everyone wants to change their personality. Recent research at the University of Illinois proves this. Over 90 percent of people report being dissatisfied with at least some aspect of their personality, which they hope to improve for the better.

Despite wanting to change, people have been led to believe they can't. Many popular schools of psychology argue that personality is innate, immutable, and fixed.

The reason personality is viewed as fixed is because, as a rule, psychologists place extreme emphasis and value on the past. A core tenet of many personality theories is that *the past is the greatest predictor of the future.* This comes from the common viewpoint of "causal determinism," the idea that everything that happens or exists is caused by prior conditions or events. From this view, people are *caused* by prior events, like one domino in a toppling chain.

The word "caused" here is extreme: not "influenced" or "guided," but "caused." Being "caused" by the past means you have no choice or possibility in the matter of who you are and what you can do. Instead, you're forced to accept whatever personality you have been dealt. Who you are right now is simply a domino being toppled over by your past experiences. You can't change the past. You can only *discover* and better understand who you *really* are and why.

This is why people seek to discover or "find" themselves. They are looking for who "they" are. For most, the notion that you can imagine and create yourself and your own personality almost sounds ridiculous, like magical thinking.

But does it have to be this way? Is your personality actually fixed and unchangeable?

No, it's not. And there is a lot of data, especially newly unearthed data, that proves this.

If you're someone who's tried making big changes in your life but feel stuck or discouraged, then this book is for you. The argument of this book is that your "personality" *doesn't matter*. Even more, your personality is *not* the most fundamental aspect of who you are. Instead, your personality is *surface-level*, transitory, and a by-product of something much deeper.

The most fundamental aspect of your humanity is your ability to make choices and stand by those choices, what Viktor Frankl called the last of human freedoms, "To choose one's own way." Choosing your own way has at least two key meanings: making decisions about what you want to happen and choosing how you respond to what does happen. Choosing one's own way is what makes one human—and the more you own the power of your own decision-making, the more your life and outcomes will be within your control.

Making decisions and "choosing your own way" are not necessarily easy. There are constraints that both limit and heavily influence your ability to make choices. The two most crucial factors influencing your ability to make choices are your social and cultural environments, as well as your emotional development as a person. The more emotionally evolved you become, the less defined you'll be by your past and the less constrained you'll be by your circumstances.

Instead of being fixed, *you will be flexible.* Instead of avoiding or suppressing emotions, you'll embrace and be transformed through them.

You'll courageously pursue the life you *truly* want—regardless of how "impossible" or difficult it may currently seem to you or those around you. You'll deal with whatever emotions, lessons, or struggles come along the way. Through your learning and experience, you'll transform as a person. Your circumstances will change.

From this moment forward, you can forget about silly personality tests and "types." Instead, you can decide who you're committed to being and becoming.

Who you become is a choice—which *only you* can make. Albus Dumbledore, the wise wizard from J. K. Rowling's Harry Potter books, understood this. When Harry Potter was seeking guidance, trying to understand why the Sorting Hat suggested he join the Slytherin house, Dumbledore explained, "It is our choices, Harry, that show what we truly are, far more than our abilities."

Harry Potter wasn't "born" to be a Gryffindor. He didn't have the innate personality of a Gryffindor. He chose to be one, and that choice and the experiences that followed shaped his personality.

Although Dumbledore is fictional, his lesson is fundamental to understanding the truth of personality. You become who you choose to be. Yet, *fully choosing* who you are and will become is rare. We've been brainwashed into believing we don't have such a choice. Facing the responsibility and freedom of choosing your own way is, indeed, scary.

That fear and risk is why many people prefer a Sorting Hat to simply make the call for them, to decide what their destiny is. It's why people defer their decisions, potential, and identity to external measures. It's much easier emotionally to have a box to fall back on—"Oh yeah, this isn't comfortable, it must not be for me"—even if that box limits your freedom, vision, and creativity.

Creativity is risky business. It requires vulnerability and courage—with a high probability of mistakes and failures along the way. There is no guaranteed outcome with creativity and courage. Moreover, creativity can be unpredictable and take you places you didn't initially expect to go. It's not surprising, then, that most people view themselves as increasingly less creative as they age—we want things to be stable and predictable. It's also not surprising that we prefer being told what we can (and *can't*) do rather than face the risks of *creating ourselves* and our own experience.

When you decide who you'll be and the life you'll live, you can have anything you truly want. You can become an outlier. You can have experiences that not only shock other people but shock yourself. "Is this really happening to me?" will become your common experience.

Yes, it is really happening to you. Amazing, right?

You're moving forward and acting with boldness and intention. You're not limiting yourself based on what has been. You're becoming increasingly confident in your ability to see something in your mind and then watch it unfold experientially. You're seeing yourself become surrounded by others who live by creation and design, rather than default and passivity.

You don't have to be limited by what other people say you can have or achieve. If you want to be more confident and creative, or more extroverted and organized, you can become any or all of those things. If you're timid but want to become a powerful, bold, and inspirational leader, you can become that as well.

Stacy Salmon, a friend of mine, told me how she learned this truth during a Sunday school class when she was thirteen years old. As a child, Stacy had been shy, timid, and awkward. On that day, the teacher explained to the students that they could all become who they wanted to be. They could develop attributes they admired in others.

This idea sunk in for Stacy, and from that moment forward, *she stopped acting shy around others.* Stopped hiding behind her parents in social situations. Stopped awkwardly yawning to avoid attention when someone asked her a question. And in the more than twenty years since that experience, she has continually sought to develop skills, learn from others, and grow as a person. Now in her midthirties, Stacy still seeks to grow and learn, and to develop attributes and characteristics she wants or admires in others. She's no longer that shy girl. She's confident and intentional.

That's the truth of personality. It's not innate but trained. It can and does change. It can and should be chosen and designed. Choosing one's own way is a primary purpose of our lives. Yet there is a fear in making choices, because choices have consequences. As a result, people avoid making decisions, fail to choose their own way, and limit their capacity for growth, learning, and change.

Anyone who's ever done something great with their life had to transform themselves from who they were to who they became. They had to see something new in their mind and convince themselves it was possible. They had to act courageously beyond their current personality and circumstances to eventually do what they did and become who they became.

Outsiders may view the hyper-successful or influential as "different" or "special." But if you asked those who actually did it, they'd say they are quite ordinary, and that the life they created was a matter of choice.

In order to become a new person, you must have a new goal—a purpose worth pursuing. Your goal is the reason you develop new attributes and skills, and have curated transformational experiences. Without a meaningful goal, attempting change lacks meaning, requires unsustainable willpower, and ultimately leads to failure.

The Past Is Not Prologue

The only thing "special" about those who transform themselves and their lives is their view of their future. They refuse to be defined by the past. They see something different and more meaningful and they never stop fueling that vision. Every single day, they maintain their vision of faith and hope and take courageous steps in that direction, accompanied by much failure and pain. With each step forward, their confidence increases and their identity becomes more flexible and less constrained by what was.

You can be the narrator of your life's story. You don't have to be defined by your past. It doesn't matter what your past identity or outcomes were.

"What's past is prologue." That's a line from William Shakespeare's *The Tempest*, uttered by Antonio, a power-hungry, manipulative character, to argue that all that has happened previously—the "past"— has led Sebastian and himself to do what they were about to do, which was commit murder. They had no other choice, it seems. They were dominos, not agents.

People use the past as the excuse to remain stuck in habits and attitudes that keep them from growing. Additionally, like Sebastian, people often use the past as the reason for previous or continued missteps. Blaming the past means you're off the hook. You're not responsible and you have no personal agency.

But as you will find over and over in this book, your past is *not* prologue. Your past is not the defining feature of who you are. You are not "caused" by your past.

Your personality isn't permanent.

The most successful people in the world base their identity and internal narrative on their future, *not their past*. For example, Elon Musk often speaks of wanting to live out the end of his life on Mars. Human travel to Mars is not a possibility yet. But dying on Mars is the story Musk tells about his future. That is the purpose shaping his identity, actions, and decisions.

Whatever you think of him, Elon Musk is focused on where he is *going* as a person, and it's entirely in his future, not his past. His attention, energy, and narrative are based on the future he's creating. You don't hear him talking about "the PayPal days." You don't see him limited by what he's previously done or failed at. You don't even hear him mention the past unless he's explicitly asked about it.

This is how successful people live: *They become who they want to be by orienting their life toward their goals, not as a repeat of the past; by acting bravely as their future selves, not by perpetuating who they formerly were.*

This book will show you how to become who you want to be, regardless of who you've been. It will teach you everything you need to know about why people get stuck in unhealthy patterns, and will provide you with science-based, actionable strategies for proactively choosing what you want, and then creating it in your life.

In *Zen and the Art of Motorcycle Maintenance*, Robert Pirsig wrote, "Steel can be any shape you want if you are skilled enough, and any shape but the one you want if you are not."

In this book, you're going to learn how personality is shaped, and how you yourself can and should be its shaper. You'll learn to be the architect and blacksmith of your personality, and thus be enabled to forge yourself into whomever you decide to be. Specifically, *Personality Isn't Permanent* will help you:

- Discover the myths of personality that limit most people's potential.
- Decide for yourself the life you want to live, regardless of how different it is from your past or present.
- Become emotionally flexible so your past no longer defines you.
- Reframe trauma and live like everything in your life happens *for* you, not *to* you.
- Become confident enough to define your own life's purpose.
- Create a network of "empathetic witnesses" who actively encourage you to continue moving forward through your highs and lows.
- Enhance your subconscious to overcome addictions and limiting patterns.
- Redesign your environment to pull you toward your future, rather than keep you stuck in the past.

In short, this book provides you the science and strategy for never getting stuck in an identity or pattern again. You will learn the most direct, simple, and effective path to change and growth. This is a proven, scientific process that you can master and apply to your life to ensure you are never trapped or defined by your past again.

Let's be clear: Deciding and creating a bigger future isn't wishful thinking. You must face uncomfortable truths you've been avoiding, and take ownership over your life. What currently prevents your dreams from becoming reality is buried trauma keeping you trapped in your past, shutting down your confidence and imagination. Sure, trauma occurs as major, life-altering events. But more often, "trauma" is planted in minor incidents and conversations that limit your view of who you are and what you can do, creating a fixed mindset.

This can't be ignored. It must be addressed.

Moreover, you have a social environment supporting your current or past-based identity and patterns rather than pushing you to evolve and become something more.

This book will challenge you to take responsibility for yourself. The fact is, basing your life off personality tests, or any other external measure, is elementary and lazy. Sure, it's helpful when growing up to get guidance and direction, but fundamental to maturity is making your own decisions, defining a meaningful purpose for yourself, and elevating yourself and others through that purpose.

If you take the personality craze seriously, then you have already forfeited your ability to choose. You've handed over responsibility for both your past and future to something outside of yourself. Instead of seeking change, you've limited your potential for change. Instead of focusing on what you can do to enhance your life, you've merely tried to discover or understand why you're disabled or limited. Instead of improving yourself, you've submitted to simply accepting yourself for who you "really" are.

Deep down, you know that is all nonsense. Deep down, you want more for yourself. You want to believe you can make changes in your life—even radical changes. Perhaps you've given up hope that it's possible for you.

But if you truly want to change your life in powerful and deliberate ways, then this book will teach you how.

Why Listen to Dr. Benjamin Hardy?

The fact that I was a "White" according to the Color Code isn't the only thing I had working against me when I was trying to date my wife. It just so happened that Lauren's best friend married a guy who went to high school with me. He strongly advised her against dating me. And for good reason.

The person I was in high school wasn't someone I'd recommend dating or marrying either. But I wasn't at all the same person I had been back then. I didn't even feel like I was in the same universe.

Back in high school, I was a highly traumatized and confused young man. My parents divorced when I was eleven, and the pain it created led my father into a deep drug addiction. Over the course of a few years, his home became a dark and strange place, filled with other drug addicts. My younger brothers and I lived with my father until it became too unstable and unhealthy to be there. During my junior year in high school, we moved in full-time with my mom, who loved us deeply but was busy trying to run a company with her sister and support additional family members.

I was the oldest of three boys and our lives became completely unstructured and uncertain. I felt like I was standing on sand, never sure of or stable in anything around me. Naturally, I began surrounding myself with kids who were also going through trauma and confusion. Although we weren't bad kids, we often bullied and teased others. We got in quite a bit of harmless trouble. More than anything, we had no stability or foundation. We played online video games all day, skateboarded, snowboarded, and did nothing productive.

I barely graduated from high school, missing so many classes that I was required to plant a tree on the school's property and do community service to make up for my absences. The year following high school, I lived at my cousin's house and slept on his Lovesac, doing nothing with my life. I had no job and had dropped out of community college after two weeks. It was way too much for me to handle. I had no work ethic, no vision for my future, and no confidence or ability to comprehend textbooks. *World of Warcraft* was my escape.

Around age twenty, I decided to leave my hometown and serve a church mission. I was fed up with how my life was going and wanted a fresh start. This two-year experience changed everything for me. I came back a different person with enhanced capabilities and a powerful vision for my future.

My mission was the first time in my life that I felt free to be whoever I wanted to be. I wasn't constrained by my past or my environment. I had a singular focus and purpose, which allowed me to craft a new identity with new behavior and drive. I committed on my first day to be the best missionary I could be—an example and a leader. It was the perfect situation to reinvent myself.

And that's exactly what I did.

I learned how to process and transform my trauma. I did this by reading more than a hundred books, filling stacks of journals, having open conversations about my painful past with loving friends and leaders who encouraged me, and especially through serving and helping others improve their lives. I spent two years helping other people overcome their problems and saw and experienced things that completely changed how I viewed the world and life in general.

I came to grasp just how finite life is, and how coddled many are from the realities of the world.

This woke me up.

When I got home, I knew how much I'd changed and also sensed that my friends and family couldn't comprehend that change. I decided to attend a different college from my high school friends where no one knew my backstory and kept me trapped in their perceptions of my former self.

I flew through college from start to finish in three years, married my dream girl, and got accepted into a top-tier PhD program in organizational psychology. I started my PhD in the fall of 2014, and during the first year made $13,000 as a graduate administrative assistant.

In January 2015, Lauren and I became foster parents to three children—Kaleb, Jordan, and Logan. Also in early 2015, I started blogging online and sharing my insights about psychology and personal change. My work immediately took off, reaching millions of people within the first few months. Over the next three years, from 2015 to 2018, I was the number one writer in the entire world on Medium.com, one of the largest online platforms at the time.

In February 2018, after years of fighting the foster system in court, we were able to adopt Kaleb, Jordan, and Logan. Less than a month after the adoption, Lauren became pregnant with twins who were born in December of that same year. We officially went from zero to five kids in a single calendar year. It was insane. But such is the life we chose and continue to choose. Our shared vision and purpose pave the way for a very steep growth curve—not easy, but incredibly meaningful and deep.

In early 2019, I completed my PhD and my writing continues to be read by millions of people online every month. I went from a derelict sleeping on someone else's sofa to running a successful seven-figure business and being a father of five kids by doing exactly what I'm about to explain to you in this book.

Despite the fact that my work and education have shown me that people can and do change, the biggest evidence of the ideas in this book is *my own life*. I'm not trying to be a guru on a stage. I'm an ordinary person experiencing a humbling and transformative life. I want to help you do the same—whatever that means or looks like for you.

It truly doesn't matter what your past has been. It doesn't matter what some stupid personality test says or what people from your high school think about you.

What matters is *who you want to be.*

What matters are *the choices you make.*

If you've ever questioned if you can really change, the answer is *yes!*

Regardless of who you've been, you no longer have to be *that person.* As you'll soon discover, you actually aren't that person now, and you won't be that person in the future. Your personality changes over time regardless of intention. But once you make it intentional, your level of change will be dramatic and directed, not random. As the actress Lily Tomlin explained, looking back over her life and career, "I always wanted to be somebody, but now I realize I should have been more specific."

You are going to become *someone.* That much is certain. The question is: *Who are you going to be?* And how specific and intentional will you be in that creation process?

The more specific the vision, the more clear the path and the more potent the motivation. You choose your purpose and then you give your whole soul to that purpose. In due time, you'll transform.

You're the one who decides who you become. Not some personality test, and not your past.

Who will you choose to be?

This is *the* book that will show you the most effective way for intentionally and strategically becoming the person you intend and choose to be. If I've done my job, you will experience a high dose of emotions over the course of reading this book. Emotions are the doorway to change and transformation. If you experience resistance through your reading, take heart. You're on the brink of facing the truth of who you are.

Are you ready to learn the truth about personality?

Buckle your seat belts. You're bound to hear something you've never heard before. Something that could change your life.

CHAPTER 1

The Myths of Personality

> Human beings are works in progress that mistakenly think they're finished.
>
> —*Daniel Gilbert, PhD*

In 2012, Vanessa O'Brien was knee deep in mud in the middle of the Sugapa Valley jungle. She and a small band of explorers were attempting to summit the Carstensz Pyramid, which at 4,884 meters (16,024 feet) above sea level is the highest mountain on the island of New Guinea.

Pulling herself through the mud, smashing her face into hard branches, getting cut and bruised, climbing over huge trees with her five-foot, four-inch body, trying to pick herself up and immediately finding herself back in the mud facedown, Vanessa was crying.

But not just crying, she was having a full-blown emotional breakdown and identity crisis.

In the midst of this breakdown, Vanessa's psychology began to unravel. Her views of the world, including of herself, were coming apart at the seams. For someone used to succeeding, some very dark thoughts were racing through her mind:

Nothing is going to get better for me.

It just gets worse.

Every step I take feels like I'm going backward.

Everything I do is wrong.

Why can't I do this?

What the hell?!

The sheer difficulty, pain, and frustration of what Vanessa was experiencing pushed her outside her frame of reference. Everything she thought she knew now seemed wrong. Her identity wasn't as clear as it had been. The world and life felt confused.

All she could feel was pain and torture.

Her ego and identity cracked wide open. The result of this experience—which ultimately ended in the successful summit—was that she was no longer the same person.

Oliver Wendell Holmes Jr. said, "A mind that is stretched by a new experience can never go back to its old dimensions."

For Vanessa O'Brien, having her mind and identity stretched wasn't a singular event but a common occurrence over the course of a decade.

For most of Vanessa's life, she was commonly considered a type A personality. In 2009, she was working successfully in the financial industry. A career-driven woman, she would describe her life as "very predictable." Not much deviated in her world.

The only thing Vanessa really thought about was her work and getting to the next rung on the corporate ladder. Her greatest excitement was the two-week vacations she took with her husband every year, where they'd sightsee and scuba dive.

Fast forward to 2019 and Vanessa has a completely different personality. No longer does her life fit within the narrow confines of her career-driven goals. Rather than being what she would consider "career" or even "goal" driven, she is now "purpose-driven."

If you had a conversation with Vanessa in 2009, you would have heard a lot about her career. She probably wouldn't have asked you any questions about yourself. If you weren't in the financial industry, there wouldn't be much the two of you could discuss. You'd likely be uninteresting to her. Given that her work was her life, she wouldn't give you much time because she was pretty busy.

If you had a conversation with Vanessa in 2019, you'd hear a lot about the state of the planet. You'd hear about glaciers melting. You'd hear about human potential and about how not only do we as people have the capability to change our lives, we have the responsibility to save our planet.

During that conversation, Vanessa would ask lots of questions about *you*. She'd be interested in what's important to you and what drives you. She'd be willing and open to answer your questions. She wouldn't be in a hurry, but totally present and in the moment. You'd feel inspired and at peace in her presence.

If Vanessa were to take a personality test in 2009, all of her responses would be self-focused and targeted around her only priority in life, her career. She would score very high on conscientiousness and extroversion and she would score low on openness to new experiences, agreeableness, and neuroticism.

Personality tests are generally self-reported. And it's likely that Vanessa would view herself as emotionally stable, given that she rarely put herself outside her comfort zone. As she herself stated, her life and routine were highly predictable. Moreover, Vanessa would also likely view herself as extroverted, given the social requirements of climbing the corporate ladder.

Rather than being self-absorbed, the 2019 Vanessa is far more others-oriented. She used to desire being the spotlight and the star.

Now she'd rather be at the tail end of her group on a big climb, ensuring that everyone on her team safely makes it to the top. Rather than having a well-trodden path to her future as the linear-thinking and ladder-climbing 2009 Vanessa, the 2019 Vanessa would describe her future as more "uncertain."

It's not that she doesn't have goals or ambitions. Her goals are actually bigger and her purpose clearer than ever. However, her goals aren't already carved out for her. Rather than ascending a single humdrum path, Vanessa now horizontally crosses multiple boundaries on a path she herself is blazing.

She is charting territories that not only she but no one else has charted before. She's constantly taking on new challenges and trying things for the first time in her life. For example, she's currently writing her autobiography, detailing the story of how she went from corporate ladder climber to world-renowned mountain climber holding multiple Guinness World Records. She's leading and is involved in multiple organizations. She travels the world giving talks.

Her fascinating and exciting life isn't all laughter and sunshine. By constantly engaging in work and activities that are new and different, she experiences a much wider spectrum of emotions. Some days are extremely painful, complex, and confusing. Other days, though, like when she's out in the mountains, can only be described as ecstasy, deeply meaningful, and undefinable bliss.

Thus, if Vanessa were to take a five-factor personality test in 2019, her responses would be very different from her 2009 self. Having given up her path of achieving narrowly defined career goals in favor of taking on new challenges and pushing herself past her limits, she would likely score higher on neuroticism, openness to new experience, and agreeableness, and lower on conscientiousness and extroversion. She treasures her solace now more than ever, despite being more and better connected to others.

Remember, personality tests are *self-reported*. Our view of ourselves is constantly changing based on our current focus, context, and emotions.

Vanessa's life is far from the predictable and consistent one it once was, and that has made her a more fluid, open, and adaptable person. Her big-picture purpose has her involved in activities, projects, relationships, and situations she could not have initially planned for. But she's committed—fiercely committed—and thus willing to do whatever it takes to move her purpose forward.

Vanessa's *purpose*, not her personality, is the determining factor in what she can do and what she does do. Moreover, in relentlessly pursuing her purpose, her personality has changed dramatically and will continue to change.

According to the futurist, author, and founder of XPRIZE, Peter Diamandis, "A single individual driven by a purpose can change the world. And you can change the world. I truly believe that."

Diamandis calls this "MTP," or "Massively Transformative Purpose." The idea is simple: You have a purpose so big and inspiring that pursuing it transforms your entire life. You're the one who selects and chooses that purpose. You invest yourself in it. You shout it from the rooftops. You change yourself and your life for it. You improve the world through it. From Diamandis's perspective, and mine, you can and should have a personal MTP, as well as a professional or organizational one.

A single day in Vanessa's 2019 life would be unfathomable to 2009 Vanessa. What is "normal" to 2019 Vanessa would be incredibly *uncomfortable*, and likely even unattractive or uninteresting, to 2009

Vanessa. From 2019 Vanessa's perspective, she can barely even relate to her former self. Even still, she is empathetic and grateful to her former self, and humbled by her future.

Now all Vanessa wants to do is contribute, serve, and connect. She's far kinder, more focused on other people, more flexible and patient, and more focused on what she considers the big picture. When I asked her who she sees as her *future self,* she said she sees herself as a philanthropist.

How did this happen? How did Vanessa O'Brien go from a self-absorbed type A corporate desk jockey to an adventurer, philosopher, and philanthropist, interested in saving the planet?

How did she transform from someone who didn't take on significant physical challenges to becoming the first American and British (she has dual citizenship and thus qualifies for both) woman to climb K2, which at 8,611 meters (28,251 feet) above sea level is the second-highest mountain in the world, and harder to ascend than Everest?

How did she become someone who received the Explorer of the Year award in 2018 from the Scientific Exploration Society and the Fearless Girl award in 2019 from New York congresswoman Carolyn Maloney?

How was she able to set the Guinness World Record for climbing the highest peak on every continent in 295 days, the fastest time by any woman?

How was she able to become purpose-driven and interested and caring toward other people?

How was she able to become kinder, more considerate, more philosophical, and more conscious about herself and reality?

If you sat Vanessa down with some of her colleagues from the financial industry, they'd be shocked by what she's done over the previous decade and who she's become.

But how did this all happen?

It really comes down to a few key things.

Vanessa's change started with the market crash of 2008. Given the change in context, she and her husband decided to move to a new country and start fresh. The pain of the market crash and the confusion it caused led her to question what really mattered to her. She decided she needed a new purpose in life, something that would give her more meaning.

With the help of some friends, she selected a new and challenging goal: to climb Mount Everest. Through the process and pain of achieving that goal—as well as some humbling failures along the way—her identity, personality, and views of the world changed, leading to other goals and pursuits.

Over the ten years following, she continuously pursued bigger and more challenging goals, which led to experiences that altered her identity, perspective, and purpose. Through her experiences, her expectations were often shattered, causing her to rethink her former views. As she put it, "Often, those who you'd expect the most from give the least and those you expect the least from give the most."

Vanessa has let go of her past. Her ego that was once tied to her salary, her title, and her material possessions has been destroyed. She's embraced a massively transformative and meaningful purpose in her life. She is now focused on the future, and in doing as much good as she possibly can. She cares less about what others think of her.

Because of these extreme changes, Vanessa is what personality psychologists would call an *outlier*. Some might even diagnose her with a personality disorder. But really, she is not so different a person from you or me. Yes, she has done incredible, exceptional things, but it would be a mistake to think she is somehow inherently different, or a freak exception to a rule.

She isn't "special" or "different." She's actually ordinary, but has chosen to become extraordinary, exposing the lie that our personality is innate, stable, and consistent over our lives. Indeed, the science of personality and our own lives tell a completely different story from what many of us have been told.

The average person's personality may not change as drastically as Vanessa O'Brien's has, given that few would proactively put themselves through the physical and emotional rigors Vanessa has. But everyone's personality is going to change, *and indeed has already changed.*

Personality is not stable but changes regardless of whether you're purposeful about that change or not.

In fact, psychologists agree that you shouldn't be surprised to get different test scores on the same personality test at different times or even in different settings.

Personality, it turns out, is far more dynamic and malleable than was previously thought. Despite this fact, and the growing body of science that proves it, many psychologists and the general public continue to see personality from the perspective of the 1960s, '70s, and '80s—as a fixed and unalterable *trait*. Many Baby Boomers, who grew up in a culture emphasizing "traits," still hold to the views that people are born "hardwired" at birth. This culture of traits is easily evidenced by the leadership dynamics of that era—white, male, tall, etc. It often manifests as racism.

Emerging science and a changing world prove the opposite.

People can and do change.

A lot.

And in a world where information, travel, connection, and experience are easier to get than ever before, many of the constraints of previous generations are gone. Choice is far more abundant, even overabundant. And as a result, responsibility for choice, and who we become as individuals and societies, is far higher.

This chapter's job, then, is to debunk the pervasive and destructive myths about personality, which are:

1. Personality can be categorized into "types."
2. Personality is innate and fixed.
3. Personality comes from your past.
4. Personality must be discovered.
5. Personality is your true and "authentic" self.

These dominant views, although potentially helpful in one's formative years, are ultimately destructive. They lead people to adopt a narrow and fixed mindset about themselves. They lead people on a misguided hunt to "discover" their "true" selves, which, for most, is an indecisive journey to mediocrity.

As a human being, it is your responsibility to create yourself through the decisions you make and the environments you choose. And as you'll find, you have been creating yourself all along, even if unintentionally.

After debunking the five myths and rejecting them with science and common sense, I'll walk you through an accurate and useful view of personality in chapter 2, empowering you to take your personality—as well as your own past and future—squarely into your own hands. The remainder of the book will teach you how to become the person you want to be.

Myth #1: Personality Can Be Categorized into "Types"

> There is no such thing as a pure extrovert or a pure introvert. Such a man would be in the lunatic asylum.
>
> *—Dr. Carl Jung*

There are two types of people in the world: those who believe there are two types of people in the world, and those who don't.

According to the Myers-Briggs, however, there are actually *sixteen* types of people in the world.

But wait, according to the Revised NEO Personality Inventory, there are only *six* types of people.

For me, though, there are only four types of people in this world: Hufflepuffs, Gryffindors, Slytherins, and Ravenclaws.

So, what gives?

Are there two types of people in the world? Are there four? Are there six? Or is it sixteen?

The first myth of personality is that there are personality "types." There is *no such thing* as a personality type. Personality types are social or mental constructions, not actual realities. The notion is a surface-level, discriminative, dehumanizing, and horribly inaccurate way of looking at the complexity of what is a human being.

There is no science behind the idea of personality types, and most of the popular personality quizzes were actually created by people who had no business trying to define people.

In the 2018 book *The Personality Brokers: The Strange History of Myers-Briggs and the Birth of Personality Testing*, Dr. Merve Emre explains that personality testing has become a $2 billion industry, with the Myers-Briggs test being the most popular of them all. Interestingly, neither Katharine Briggs nor her daughter, Isabel Myers, had any training in psychology, psychiatry, or testing. Neither ever worked in a laboratory or an academic institution. Since access to universities for women was limited, the two developed their system from home, instead of in a lab or at a university.

Katharine Briggs used her experience as a wife and mother, not science or psychology, to develop her theories in the early 1900s. Noticing that she and her spouse responded differently to life, and that one child was more reclusive than the other, she wanted to devise a system that accounted for social nuances.

According to Briggs, a person can put themselves through a lot of psychological pain by trying to solve incompatibilities. Instead of trying to change oneself, Briggs proposed that the differences in how people respond to life are innate and unchangeable. They are hardwired *dispositions* to be recognized and accommodated.

No matter who you are or how you show up in life, your behavior should be accepted as "normal." That's what Briggs argued. If you're shy, people around you should account for that in how they deal with you. If you're a nervous wreck, they should make accommodations for you. If you're kind and compassionate, they should always expect you to behave in that manner.

Under this paradigm, the way you react to life is just "who you are," and you shouldn't be ashamed of it. You shouldn't try to change who you are, and you couldn't if you tried. Even if these traits are limitations, there's nothing you can do about it. Just live with the constraints God or your DNA has given you.

Although entertaining, type-based personality tests are unscientific—and would have you believe that you are essentially more limited than you really are. They portray an inaccurate and overly simplified portrait of people, filled with broad and sweeping generalizations, that anybody could feel relates to them. These tests oversimplify psychology, making people think they know more about it than they really do. Of this, Wharton business professor and organizational psychologist Dr. Adam Grant explained, "The Myers-Briggs is like asking people what do you like more: shoelaces or earrings? You tend to infer that there's going to be an 'aha!' even though it's not a valid question. . . . [It] creates the illusion of expertise about psychology."

We've got an entire generation of social media personality gurus who can tell you anything and everything about you, from who you should date and marry to whether you should have kids or not to what you should do for work, and whether or not you'll be successful and happy—all based on your score on a particular test. It *feels* scientific, but really it's just superstition dressed up as science.

In social science, there are four standards to determine the merit of a proposed theory: Are the categories (1) reliable, (2) valid, (3) independent, and (4) comprehensive? For the Myers-Briggs Type Indicator, the evidence says no, no, no, and no. The real lesson of the Myers-Briggs test is not some insight into your personality, but the incredible power of marketing. That's the real brilliance of Myers-Briggs.

Although there remains disagreement among psychologists regarding whether personality can change or not, there is agreement that personality tests such as Myers-Briggs should not be taken seriously for the four reasons just listed. And that "personality types" as popularized by such tests and pop psychologists don't actually exist.

When done intentionally and strategically, defining yourself as a certain "type" of person, or *giving yourself* a specific label, may be useful. For instance, Jeff Goins had always wanted to be a writer, but hadn't done anything about it. Yet, when he labeled himself as a "writer," that identification bolstered him to start writing, and, ultimately, to become a successful author. Thus, Goins was intentional about the label he chose, and that label helped him achieve his goals.

Labels can serve goals, but goals should never serve labels. When a goal serves a label, you've made the label your ultimate reality, and you've created a life to prove or support that label. You see this when someone says, "I'm pursuing this because I'm an extrovert." This form of goal-setting occurs when you base your goals on your current persona rather than setting goals that expand upon and change who you are.

Your personality should come *from* your goals. Your goals shouldn't come from your personality. Paul Graham—the entrepreneur, venture capitalist, and author—wrote, "The more labels you have for yourself, the dumber they make you." When someone proactively labels themself an "introvert" or even an "extrovert," they've officially made themself "dumber"—unless for some reason one of those labels will enable them to achieve a particular goal.

Research shows that labeling or diagnosing can be helpful for practitioners for guiding therapy. However, these labels should rarely be given to clients. The label becomes infused as a significant aspect of the client's identity, greatly limiting their capacity to change.

Labels create tunnel vision. Assuming a label can lead you to being "mindless," stopping you from seeing all of the times the label isn't true. As Harvard psychologist and mindfulness expert Dr. Ellen Langer has said, "If something is presented as an accepted truth, alternative ways of thinking do not even come up for consideration. . . . When people are depressed they tend to believe they are depressed all the time. Mindful attention to variability shows this is not the case."

"Personality" is far more nuanced and complex than an overly simplified generalization or category. It's not an isolated trait uninfluenced by context, culture, behavior, and a thousand other factors. Of this, Dr. Katherine Rogers, a personality psychologist, said, "We know that personality doesn't work in types. . . . I wouldn't trust the Myers and Briggs to tell me any more about my personality than I would trust my horoscope."

Dr. Rogers is completely right. And this is incredibly good news! When you allow yourself to stop defining yourself as a certain "type," such as "introvert" or "extrovert," you become far more open. Your possibilities and choices expand. Your responsibility and agency increase. You can do what you want to do, regardless of how you currently see yourself.

Despite the unscientific nature of type-based personality tests, they continue to be a pervasive fad in pop culture and also in corporate America. Many people's livelihoods are on the line based on how they respond to one of these tests. Countless careers have been ruined or derailed because they weren't the right "Color" or "type" for the position or culture.

You are not a single and narrow "type" of person. In different situations and around different people, *you are different.* Your personality is dynamic, flexible, and contextual. Moreover, your personality changes throughout your life, far more than you can presently imagine.

At different stages and seasons of your life, you're going to display a different personality. Heck, over the course of a single day, you could portray dozens of different personalities. As podcaster Jordan Harbinger said in an interview, "Before coffee, I'm an INTJ. After coffee, I'm an ENTJ."

Rather than looking at personality as a "type" you fit into, view it as a continuum of behaviors and attitudes that is flexible, malleable, and based on context. The most scientifically backed theory of personality breaks it up into what are called the "five factors":

1. How open you are to learning and experiencing new things (openness to new experience)
2. How organized, motivated, and goal-directed you are (conscientiousness)
3. How energized and connected you are around other people (extroversion)
4. How friendly and optimistic you are toward other people (agreeableness)
5. How well you handle stress and other negative emotions (neuroticism)

None of these five factors are "types." Instead, we are all *somewhere on a continuum* of each of these factors based on our preferences, experience, and situation. In different situations and circumstances, you'll show up differently in all of these—sometimes for better and sometimes for worse.

For example, researchers have found strong correspondences between the demands of a social role and one's personality profile. If a particular role requires that the person be conscientious or extroverted, then she'd exhibit a much higher degree of conscientiousness or extroversion. Yet once she leaves that role and takes on another requiring less conscientiousness or extroversion, she will manifest lower levels of these "traits." Longitudinal research highlights that a person's personality can often be explained by the social roles they espoused and relinquished throughout their life stages. Thus, social role is an oft-studied and tangible predictor of personality.

Although we think of ourselves as consistent, our behavior and attitudes are often shifting. It isn't our behavior that is consistent, but rather *our view of our behavior* that makes it seem consistent. We selectively focus on what we identify with and ignore what we don't.

In the process, we often miss or purposefully disregard the many instances when we're acting out of character.

Recent research shows that people want to view themselves as more fluid and flexible, and have specific desires to improve their personality. Less than 13 percent of people reported being satisfied with themselves as they are. Generally, they wanted to score higher on openness, conscientiousness, and extroversion. They wanted to score lower on neuroticism.

For those interested in improving themselves for a specific reason, recent science shows that such changes are possible. A 2015 study by Drs. Nathan Hudson and Chris Fraley showed that personality can be intentionally changed through goal-setting and sustained personal effort. Research from Drs. Christopher Soto and Jule Specht shows that personality changes accelerate when people are leading meaningful and satisfying lives.

Each of the five factors *will change* over your lifetime whether you attempt to change them or not, but you certainly can consciously change any and all of them. Vanessa O'Brien set the goal of climbing Mount Everest, and that goal led her to being more open to new experiences.

It should be noted that current and developing research on personality flexibility is conservative in expected change, at least in the short term. However, as will be shown throughout this book, the depth of change is not due to impossibility. Rather, people *on average* don't make incredible and purposeful changes due to emotional and situational reasons, both of which are controllable.

Intentional change is emotionally rigorous—it doesn't exactly feel good and can even be shockingly painful. If you're unwilling to put yourself through emotional experiences, shift your perspective, and make purposeful changes to your behavior and environment, then don't expect huge changes (at least in the short run). Becoming psychologically flexible is key to personal transformation, not over-attaching to your current identity or perspectives. Becoming insatiably committed to a future purpose and embracing emotions rather than avoiding them is how radical change occurs.

Extreme change is more than possible. Indeed, all of the five factors are behaviors and, really, all are learnable *skills*. You can learn to become more open to new experiences, just as you can actually learn to become less open. You can learn to become more organized and goal-focused. You can learn to become more introverted or extroverted. You can learn to be better at relating to different types of people. You can become more emotionally intelligent rather than reactive and victim-oriented.

Perhaps the most damaging aspect of putting people into categories or types is that such categories can be viewed as innate and un-alterable. When you see people as being incapable of change, you begin to define them by their past. If someone has done something in the past, you view them as being a certain type of person who will always do that kind of thing rather than recognize that they may have changed.

The limitations of this view are brilliantly explored in the French novel *Les Misérables* by Victor Hugo. The novel tells the story of two people—Javert, the self-righteous police officer who believes people cannot change, and Jean Valjean, an ex-criminal who changes his life and dedicates himself to a higher and holier way. Javert cannot accept that Valjean has truly changed. In Javert's mind, a person should never be forgiven for past deeds. If a person has done wrong, he believes they are fundamentally bad.

Throughout the novel, Javert and Valjean encounter one another in various situations. It becomes Javert's obsession to bring Valjean to justice. All the while, Valjean is simply trying to live a life redeemed of his criminal past, one in which he helps other people who are struggling. In the end, Javert commits suicide because he cannot reconcile the contradiction that is Jean Valjean. Instead of changing his mind, he kills himself.

So, where are you?

In what ways have you defined yourself or others by what was done in the past?

Have you limited and overly defined yourself by categorizing or typifying yourself?

What would happen if you stopped boxing yourself into a category and opened yourself to the possibility of change?

Myth #2: Personality Is Innate and Fixed

In a recently published longitudinal study spanning more than sixty years, researchers were flummoxed by what they found. The personalities of nearly everyone in the study were *completely different* than the researchers expected.

The study began with data from a 1950s survey of 1,208 fourteen-year-olds in Scotland. Teachers were asked to use six questionnaires to rate the teenagers on six personality traits: self-confidence, perseverance, stability of mood, conscientiousness, originality, and desire to learn.

More than sixty years later, researchers retested 674 of the original participants. This time, at seventy-seven years old, the participants rated themselves on the six personality traits, and also nominated a close friend or relative to do the same. There was little to no overlap from the questionnaires taken sixty-three years earlier. As the researchers state, "We hypothesized that we would find evidence of personality stability over an even longer period of 63 years, but our correlations did not support this hypothesis."

This is the way academics say, "We were totally wrong about everything." Personality changes over time.

Longitudinal studies are incredibly difficult to perform, so they are rarely done. In the unusual instances where a follow-up test is administered to study participants, it is usually within a few weeks or months. Under these conditions, it would be easy to conclude that personality rarely changes. If you were to take the same personality test three or six months apart, you'd likely get a similar score, unless something drastic happened during those few months.

The longer the interval between tests, the more different the outputs will be. As the researchers of the sixty-three-year study further concede, "Our results suggest that, when the interval is increased to as much as 63 years, there is hardly any relationship at all."

Not only does your personality change over time but it changes far more than you'd expect. According to research done by Harvard psychologist Dr. Daniel Gilbert, over a ten-year period of time, *you're not going to be the same person.*

In his research, Dr. Gilbert asked people how much their interests, goals, and values had changed over the previous decade. He then asked them how much they expected their interests, goals, and values to change over the next ten years.

What Dr. Gilbert found is that when asked to analyze the difference between their former and current selves, people can easily recognize changes in their personality over the previous ten years. Even still, people consistently expect only *minor changes* to occur over the next decade.

In psychology, the name for this phenomenon is the "end-of-history illusion," and it occurs in people of all ages who believe they have experienced significant personal growth and changes up to the present moment but will not substantially grow or mature in the future.

As Gilbert says, "Human beings are works in progress that mistakenly think they're finished."

Human beings have a weird way of thinking that who we are in the present moment is the "arrived," "finished," and "evolved" version of ourselves. This is why, regardless of the evidence of change from our former to our present selves, we still often *feel* like the same person. In the present, we always feel like "ourselves," despite the fact that our consistent emotions and behaviors—even our habits and environment—are *entirely different* from what they were years ago.

We are highly adaptive. Even after going through extreme change, we quickly adapt to that change and it becomes our new norm. Hence, we may feel like the same person as we age and gradually change, *but we aren't actually the same.* Life is "normal," but not compared to what it was before.

An obvious way to see that our personality has changed over time is how we respond to our previous decisions. People often remove tattoos their former selves thought were a good idea. People divorce partners their former selves assumed they'd always love. People work hard to lose belly fat their former selves had no problem eating to gain. People quit jobs they were desperate to get.

People often make decisions their future selves aren't happy with because, as a rule, we aren't very good at predicting our own future. It's not that we can't predict our future but that we don't.

It's harder to imagine the future we want than to remember the past we've lived through. Imagination is a skill to be developed, one that few adults truly master. Instead, adults become less creative and imaginative as they age, and increasingly fixed and dogmatic in their narrow viewpoints.

Quick question: How much time do you spend imagining your future self?

For most people, the answer is not very much.

What I've just described are two major obstacles that prevent people from predicting and creating their future personality:

1. We assume our present personality is a finished product (the end-of-history illusion).
2. We overemphasize the importance of the past, which leads us to become increasingly narrow in how we view ourselves and the world.

Your personality changes. It has changed and it will continue changing in the future. Consequently, it's time to start thinking about who your future self is going to be. *You don't want to be surprised, disappointed, or frustrated by where you're at and who you become.* You don't want to leave your future self hanging due to neglect, bad planning, or poor decisions on the part of your present self.

It's best to make decisions based on what your future, not your present, self wants. It's best to decide and act from the vantage point of your desired circumstances, not your present ones. As American jurist and religious leader Dallin Oaks said:

> We make countless choices in life, some large and some seemingly small. Looking back, we can see what a great difference some of our choices made in our lives. We make better choices and decisions if we look at the alternatives and ponder where they will lead. . . . Our present and our future will be happier if we are always conscious of the future. . . . "Where will this lead?" is also important in choosing how we label or think of ourselves. . . . Don't choose to label yourselves or think of yourselves in terms that put a limit on a goal for which you might strive.

The first step of this imaginative process is to distinguish your present self from your future self.

They aren't the same person.

Your future self will be a different person from whom you currently are. It's bad for decision-making to assume your future self will be the same person you are now. Of this, identity researcher Dr. Hal Hershfield said, "The analogy of the future self as another person may seem like a strange one, but it is rather powerful when it comes to understanding long-term decision-making."

Who you want to be in the future is *more important* than who you are now, and should actually inform who you are now. Your intended future self should direct your current identity and personality far more than your former self does.

Hopefully, your future self will be far wiser and have a far wider range of experiences than your current self. Your future self will have greater opportunities, deeper relationships, and a better self-view. Hopefully, your future self will have greater agency and choice than your current self, with more knowledge, skills, and connections.

It's also possible that your future self could be *more limited* than your current self, depending on what you do in the here and now. If you engage in unhealthy behaviors, make terrible choices, or develop bad habits, then your future self will have *less freedom* than your current self. Sometimes, things that seem small and harmless—like watching YouTube videos before bed, or having an extra drink at the bar—can cascade and compound into huge problems over time.

I'm sad to say that some of my own friends and extended family members are now in terrible situations due to their own poor decisions. Their life isn't how their former selves thought it would go, not due to some freak accident but to their own lack of intention, planning, and goal-directed action. They got lax, and now they're paying the price. And it's not just their situation that is worse but they themselves—their personality, views, and relationships—are far worse than what they once were.

Life starts taking on a whole new meaning when you begin thinking *right now* what your future self will want. Rather than making decisions based on your current identity, you could begin making decisions your future self would love and appreciate.

It's your responsibility to set your future self up for as much opportunity, success, and joy as possible. This is how you become the person and create the life you want, rather than becoming someone with regret.

Describe your future self.

Who is your future self?

How often do you imagine and consciously design your future identity?

What would happen if you based your identity on who you want to be, rather than who you've been?

Myth #3: Personality Comes from Your Past

Because sometimes the past deserves a second chance.

—*Malcolm Gladwell*

A common scientific premise of many theories is known as "causal determinism"—the idea that everything that happens or exists is caused by antecedent conditions or events. From this view, people are determined—not influenced—by prior events, like one domino in a toppling chain.

In looking at human behavior, psychologists have come to agree that the best way to predict future behavior is by looking at past behavior. And for the most part, that perspective is validated over and over. Indeed, people seem quite predictable over time.

The important question is, *Why*?

A dominant view of predictable behavior is that "personality" is a stable "trait" that is for the most part unchangeable. However, as will be shown throughout this book, this explanation is a gross and inaccurate oversimplification, which ultimately leads to mindlessness, justification, and a lack of radical progress and intentional living.

Yes, people's behavior can appear to be, and often is, predictable and consistent over time. But the reason for that consistency is not a fixed and unalterable personality. Instead, there are four far deeper reasons, which keep people stuck in patterns:

- They continue to be defined by **past traumas** that haven't been reframed.
- They have an **identity narrative** based on the past, not the future.
- Their **subconscious** keeps them consistent with their former self and emotions.
- They have an **environment** supporting their current rather than future identity.

These are the levers that drive personality—and whether you realize it or not, you can control them. When you change, reframe, or manage these levers, your personality and life can change in intentional and remarkable ways.

It's up to you whether you allow these four levers to hold you hostage—keeping you stuck and making change feel nearly impossible—or whether you utilize them to become the person you want to be.

Throughout this book, I'll show you how each of these four levers impacts your personality and suggest strategies for leveraging each lever intelligently. You'll be equipped to control these levers rather than be controlled by them, so you can become who you choose to be rather than what former experiences or "life" has led you to be.

For now, let's look at some stories and science that should shift your perspective on whether your past truly does "cause" your present.

Tucker Max is the cofounder of a successful publishing and media company, a husband, and a father of three children. Today, his family is the most important thing in the world to him. But in 2006, when he was a different person, he published a book called *I Hope They Serve Beer in Hell*. It instantly took off, became a number one *New York Times* bestseller, and sold millions of copies.

The book, as well as other books that followed, recount the repetitive nights of Max's twenties and early thirties that were filled with excessive drinking, sex with a succession of random strangers, acting cocky and belligerent to anyone who came across him, and saying the most malicious and sexually degrading things to everyone around him, both men and women.

Due to the major success of the book as well as Max's surging fame, *I Hope They Serve Beer in Hell* was made into a major motion picture and released in 2009. Expectations for the film were high, and despite criticism of his style and attitude, Max felt validated by his success and the expectations riding on the film. But upon release, the film bombed badly at the box office, and was universally panned by critics as one of the worst films of that year.

Nearly a decade later, in a 2018 interview with Tom Bilyeu, Tucker explained the film's failure as one of the worst experiences of his life, and by far one of his greatest disappointments. The sheer pain of the experience ultimately led him to finally face the demons he'd been running from his entire life.

His ego had been cracked wide open, leaving him vulnerable and unsettled. It forced him to admit, *to himself,* that he wasn't happy.

In 2012, after three years of therapy, self-reflection, honesty, and change following the movie's failure, Tucker Max released a public statement via an interview on *Forbes* stating that he was officially putting his former lifestyle behind him: "I publicly, explicitly retire. I want to be free to move on with my life, and I think the way I have to do that is to set a public end to this."

When you talk to Tucker today about his former life, he isn't bitter, angry, or embarrassed. He told me that whenever he reads his former writings, it's like reading the words of a *completely different person*. A clear sign of his own emotional healing is that his own past is viewed empathetically and even *positively*, not negatively.

"When I think about the person I was, I feel bad for that guy," Tucker told me. "I can now understand why he was acting the way he was. I feel extreme compassion for him."

This, more than anything else you'll find in this book, is what's most incredible, hopeful, and redemptive: that when you begin actively and intentionally moving forward in your life, not only does your future get better *but your past does as well*. Your past increasingly becomes something happening *for* you, not to you.

Tucker's "failure," although tortuous in the moment, was exactly what he needed. It happened for him, not to him. And since then, it has led him to having a much higher and empowering purpose for his life.

As you truly learn and have new experiences, you begin to see and interpret your past in new ways. If your view of your own past hasn't changed much over recent months or years, then you haven't learned from your past experiences and you're not actively learning now.

An unchanging past is a sure sign of emotional detachment and rigidity—an avoidance of facing the truth and moving forward in your life. The more mature you become as a person, the more differently you'll view prior experiences. I've recently been humbled by how I acted, even last year, in my business and relationships.

Your past can change, and it must change.

Your past evolves *as you evolve*.

In order to understand how the past changes, you need to know a little bit about how your memory works, and even how "history" works in general.

History is constantly being altered and revised based on who's telling the story and how far back in time it was. For example, if you read a history book written in the United States from the 1950s on the origins of the Cold War, you'd get a definitive answer backed with extensive evidence that Soviet Russia was to blame. The book would refer to Stalin's takeover of Eastern Europe, his refusal to grant the democracy he had promised his people, and his desire to spread communism to all corners of the globe.

If you picked up a US history book from the late 1960s, though, you'd likely read a different tale. You'd read of America's desire to capture economic control of Europe to secure the dollar's role in those countries. You'd read of Truman's forcefulness at the Potsdam Conference and his use of the atom bomb. Rather than Russia being responsible, you'd learn that responsibility for the Cold War was actually Washington's, and that Stalin merely acted defensively after having lost over twenty million people as a consequence of the Second World War.

By the 1980s and '90s, the story would be retold afresh from a new perspective. Historians would argue that the Cold War was unavoidable given the ideological differences existing between East and West. You'd read of the futility of placing blame on one person or even one country in particular.

Like history, which constantly changes with time and perspective, our own personal narratives also adapt or change over time and with each retelling. One reason for this is that your memory is not an inert filing cabinet. Instead, it is fluid and constantly changing as you have new experiences. In fact, your memory changes by simply recalling a particular memory. Each is a web of connections, and when a new connection is integrated into a memory, the whole of the memory changes instantly and imperceptibly.

The more times a particular story is told, the more altered that story becomes. As time goes on and culture shifts, our view of history and particular events shifts as well. So too with memory. The past, and how we view it, is more a reflection of *where we currently are* than of the past itself. As the psychologist Dr. Brent Slife states in the book *Time and Psychological Explanation*:

> We reinterpret or reconstruct our memory in light of what our mental set is in the present. In this sense, *it is more accurate to say the present causes the meaning of the past, than it is to say that the past causes the meaning of the present* [italics mine]. . . . Our memories are not "stored" and "objective" entities but living parts of ourselves in the present. This is the reason our present moods and future goals so affect our memories.

This idea that our present shapes the meaning of the past may not initially make sense. But as you'll soon see, it's actually not that complex. For instance, imagine getting to work one morning and being called in to meet with your boss. Surprisingly, and seemingly out of the blue, she offers you a 10 percent raise. You're thrilled! You walk out of her office on cloud nine.

During lunch that same day, you share the good news with your colleague who holds a similar position. She then informs you that she too got a raise earlier that day, but her raise was 15 percent.

How are you feeling with that new information? Still on cloud nine? For most people, probably not.

Why not, though? The 10 percent raise *didn't change* . . . but the meaning of it did.

The new context changed everything. Ten percent, by itself, doesn't actually mean much. It only means what it is contrasted against. Before, you were contrasting your 10 percent raise with your former income. Now you're contrasting it against your colleague's 15 percent raise.

The present context shifted the meaning of the past. This truth is embodied in a quote by Saadi Shirazi, who said, "I cried because I had no shoes until I met a man who had no feet." No shoes is relative.

Context changes everything. Personality tests ignore context by assuming "you" *are* your score in every context.

Context also changes memory. The content of the memory changes because, like a recipe, more has been added in. Thus, new experiences alter former memories, adding new perspective and meaning to those memories. Sometimes, new experiences can lead to the entire forgetting of former experiences.

Our past, like our personality, is not unchanging and fixed. It is far more about *context* than content. Context is always superior to content because it determines the meaning, focus, emphasis, and even appearance of the content. When you change the context, you simultaneously change the content!

Just because something happened in the past doesn't mean the event or experience is "objective." This can be a bitter pill to swallow, especially for people who insist on the past or specific events being understood a particular way.

Our past, like any experience or event, is a subjective perspective, which we ourselves ascribe meaning to—whether positive or negative, good or bad. Without question, experiences from our past can and do impact us. But it isn't actually our past that is impacting us, but our present interpretation and emotional attachment *to that past*.

To say, "That's just the way I am because of my past" is to declare you're emotionally stuck in your past.

Trauma can and does happen to all of us, both in large and small degrees. When our trauma is unresolved, we stop moving forward in our lives. We become emotionally rigid and shut off, and thus stop learning, evolving, and changing. As such, our past becomes rigid as well, and our memory persists in an unchanging and painful way.

By continually avoiding our past traumas and the emotions they create, our life becomes an unhealthy and repetitive pattern. When this is the case, then, yes, our past does become an accurate predictor of our future. It's not because personality is unchanging, but rather because we're avoiding that change. Lessons are repeated, learned.

A clear indicator that someone has unresolved trauma is that his life and personality are repetitive for an extended period. But as he faces, opens up about, becomes more aware of, and ultimately reframes his trauma, he allows himself to take a positive and mature view of his past. His present and future will then stop reflecting his past.

Tucker Max views his former self with compassion and greater understanding. He no longer *identifies* with his former self. They are two totally different people with different values, goals, and context. And although Tucker wouldn't necessarily want to be his former self, he has empathy toward that person and others like him.

Tucker's view of previous events continues to evolve as he evolves. He is not the victim of his past. His past isn't causing him to be the way he presently is. Instead, the meaning of his past continues to expand and change because he chooses not to be stuck there.

Tucker chose to move forward in his life, and continues to do so. He's learning, having new experiences, and integrating his experiences to evolve himself and the meaning of his life. Increasingly, Max's *future self,* which includes his values and his family, is who is pulling his present self forward.

Therefore, it is foolish to say that Tucker's past is what is causing him to be who he is. In fact, his past is *continually changing* in light of who he is becoming.

The same is true of you and me.

How we describe, interpret, and identify with our past has far more to do with where we are, here and now, than it has to do with our actual past.

If you're still angry with your parents for your childhood, for example, this speaks more to who you *currently are* than what actually happened in your childhood. To continue blaming any person or event from the past makes you the victim, and reflects more on you than whoever or whatever it is you're blaming.

I don't want to nor am I trying to discount your experiences in any way. Perhaps you have lived through some truly horrific events. Perhaps you saw things you believe you can never unsee. Such experiences may have been extremely difficult to deal with, potentially leaving you feeling misunderstood and alone.

But "changing your past" doesn't mean you should change or discount the content of any of those experiences! They can actually be a gold mine of insights, meaning, and possibility.

It isn't the contents of your past that need changing, *but how you view them today*. As Marcel Proust said, "The real voyage of discovery consists not in seeking new landscapes, but in having new eyes." It's not about seeing a million things, but being able to see the same things a million different ways. And hopefully in better and more useful ways.

Viewing your past in more effective and healthy ways is a natural aspect of evolving as a person. Seeking new experiences is an essential and powerful part of this evolution. However, far too often, people fail to learn from or be transformed by their experiences. Instead, they often avoid them, or fail to learn from them as they happen.

In order to actively create new experiences and be transformed by them, you'll need to become more psychologically flexible. Psychological flexibility is the skill of being fluid and adaptive, holding your emotions loosely, and moving toward chosen goals or values. You need psychological flexibility to reframe your past and imagine a future self. The more flexible you become, the less you'll be overwhelmed or stopped by emotions. Instead, you'll embrace and learn from them.

Becoming psychologically flexible is part of becoming more emotionally evolved as a human being. Emotional development is at the core of understanding personality. The less emotionally developed and flexible a person is, the more they will avoid hard experiences. The more they'll be limited and defined by painful experiences from their past. This is counterintuitive, as many people come to believe the best way to deal with hard experiences is by burying their emotions and fighting a silent battle, alone.

You become more psychologically flexible and emotionally evolved by facing your past, head-on, and by getting help from other people. Every time you face your past, you change it. Every time you face your future with honesty and courage, you become more flexible and mature. You build confidence, which enhances your imagination. You stop being as limited by who you were and how you feel, and instead, you're enabled to be and do what you want, regardless of what is involved in being and doing it.

Emotions are the doorway to growth and learning. The reason people's personalities plateau and get stuck in repetitive cycles is because they are avoiding the difficult and challenging emotions involved in *learning* and in connecting with themselves and others. As a result, they remain weighted down by their limited perceptions of their past far longer than necessary.

So, what stories are you telling about your past self?

Who was your former self?

In what ways are you different from your former self?

How has your past changed due to more recent experiences?

How would your life be different if your past was something happening for you rather than to you?

How could life change if you embraced the truth that your former and current selves are two fundamentally different people?

How would your life be if you never again blamed or limited yourself and your future based on the past?

Myth # 4: Personality Must Be Discovered

> Life isn't about finding yourself. Life is about creating yourself.
>
> —*George Bernard Shaw*

I have a friend named Kary. She's in her early forties and has never been able to find work she can stay passionate about. Every few years, she changes industries and never drives significant change in her organization.

She's frustrated because she feels like she doesn't really know who she is. She sees a lot of her friends and colleagues who know something she doesn't. "It seems they have discovered the secret of life," she told me, "They have found and maximized their talents and passions."

Kary is still waiting to find herself. She's passive, not active, about life. She's hoping that at some point, lightning will strike, she'll have an epiphany, and *then* she'll be able to move forward with confidence. Then she'll be able to truly be who she really is.

What Kary fails to understand is that inspiration follows action, not the other way around. Lightning isn't going to strike for her. Unless and until she takes action, her confidence and imagination will remain low. She needs to *decide* what she wants and begin moving forward. With progress—even miniscule progress—her clarity and confidence will increase, opening the door for greater flexibility and change.

Kary's concern that she hasn't "found" herself or her passion isn't new or unique. Common cultural wisdom suggests that your "passion" is something you discover and then maximize. If you don't have a passion, you're a nobody. You're uninteresting. That's the message of today's pop culture, which fits nicely with our culture's obsession with personality tests. Passion is viewed as something to be *discovered* because, like personality, your passion is something assumed to be innate and unique.

In the book *So Good They Can't Ignore You,* author Cal Newport argues that rather than trying to find your passion, you should instead develop rare and valuable skills. Find a need and begin filling it. Once you've developed skills and begin seeing success, passion comes as an organic by-product, or an indirect effect. As he writes, "Passion comes after you put in the hard work to become excellent at something valuable, not before. In other words, what you do for a living is much less important than how you do it."

Newport's perspectives on passion dovetail exactly with the research on motivation. Like passion, motivation isn't something to be discovered, but to be created through proactive and forward action.

Both passion and motivation are effects, not causes. As Dr. Jerome Bruner, a Harvard psychologist, said, "You more likely to act yourself into feeling than feel yourself into action." As stated previously, confidence is the same way. You can't have it first; it must come as a by-product of chosen and goal-consistent action.

Wanting the passion first, before putting in the work, is like wanting to get paid before you begin a job. It's get-rich-quick thinking and completely lazy. It's equivalent to wanting a fully developed personality without making any effort, without being creative and taking any action or risks or going through any change. It's like a spoiled rich kid who wants everything given to them.

Passion is the prize, but you have to invest first.

Personality is no different. It is not something you discover but rather something you create through your actions and behaviors.

The idea that personality is to be discovered comes from the same faulty reasoning that personality is innate and past-based.

It's not.

Personality—like passion, inspiration, motivation, and confidence—is a by-product of your decisions in life. It's a limiting and ineffective idea to view your personality as the driving force for the decisions you make in your life, such as choosing a career you think fits your current personality.

Do you think Gandhi, Mother Teresa, or anyone else who has made a huge impact made their decisions based on their personality? Or did they make their decisions based on something much bigger, and then became who they were through their commitment to that decision?

Purpose trumps personality. Without a deep sense of purpose, your personality will be based on avoiding pain and pursuing pleasure, which is an animalistic and low-level mode of operating. This is the common view and approach to personality for most. However, when you're driven by purpose, you'll be highly flexible and you'll make decisions irrespective of pain and pleasure to create and become what you want.

Moreover, if you are serious about your purpose, it will change your personality. Your purpose isn't something you discover, but something you ultimately choose for yourself. Stop looking for it and make the choice, then allow that choice to transform you.

Rather than your decisions and goals being the by-product of your personality, your personality should become the by-product of your decisions and goals.

As you proactively and intentionally make positive decisions, develop skills, and seek out new experiences, your personality will develop and change in meaningful ways. It will adapt to the level of your goals and decisions, rather than your decisions and goals falling to the level of your current personality.

Trying to discover your personality leads to inaction, avoidance of hard conversations, distracting yourself through consumption, and making excuses for how you're currently living. It puts you in the passenger seat of your own life. Instead, you can, and should, be the driver. You can be the creator.

Another inherent problem with the view that your personality is something you discover is that it leads to very self-centered thinking. Life becomes all about you, you, you. Take, for example, the current frustration with Millennials in the workforce. Millennials, fairly or not, are viewed as lazy and entitled because they are unwilling to do anything they are not passionate about. They fall into the trap of believing their passion is something that should come immediately and instinctively, rather than through the process of developing knowledge and skills and making a contribution.

In an interview on Inside Quest, author and leadership expert Simon Sinek explained that Millennials are never satisfied in their work in part because they were raised to believe they should have anything they want, not because they earned it but simply because they want it. They were given trophies without winning. They were raised on technology and instant gratification. The power dynamic in schools and colleges changed to the point that parents would often argue with teachers about their children's grades and insist that the teachers hand out a better grade.

Getting trophies for being in last place and not taking the grades you actually earned can harm your confidence in the long term. Sinek and others argue that Millennials haven't been taught to earn what they want in life, but have come to expect it without effort. Given the lack of self-esteem and the desire for instant gratification, it makes complete sense why personality tests would be so appealing. You get an instant and easy answer without any thought or responsibility on your part.

Personality tests are fast food for the soul. They make you believe you can discover your true self in an instant. Like Katharine Briggs's suggestion that all behavior should be accommodated to, personality tests can make you feel justified by who you currently are and how you're doing in life.

You're not justified. Your personality is not discovered.

Instead of waiting for life to come to you, or for your parents or loved ones to come to your aid, why not take ownership of your own life? Why not learn how to make decisions and direct the ship of your life? Why be limited based on who you currently are? Why avoid failure and default due to a fragile identity? Why not watch yourself become someone great as a result of your own choosing and efforts?

According to Cal Newport, the idea of finding your passion is based on self-absorption. People want to find work they are passionate about because they've been taught to believe that work is all about and for them. The most successful people in the world know that work is about helping and creating value for other people. As Newport states, "If you want to love what you do, abandon the passion mindset ('what can the world offer me?') and instead adopt the craftsman mindset ('what can I offer the world?')."

There's one final problem with trying to "discover" yourself: It leads you to becoming incredibly inflexible to situations that feel difficult, complex, or outside your "innate" strengths.

Rather than adapting to difficult situations, we lazily apply labels to ourselves, such as "introvert" to justify our lack of willingness, openness, and commitment in various scenarios. As a result, we fall to the level of our labels rather than rise to the level of our commitment. In turn, we avoid conflict, difficulty, and newness, boxing ourselves into a shallow perspective of ourselves. We stunt our growth. We only do what brings instant gratification or immediate results.

Believing you must discover your personality is a *fixed mindset* that stops you from taking advantage of and creating opportunities that will transform you as a person.

In 2015, during the first year of my PhD program, my wife, Lauren, and I became foster parents of three children. We went from never having raised children before nor having done much by way of studying parenting to having three kids with attachment and other emotional needs thrown at us.

During my first year as a foster parent, I was constantly dealing with challenges that felt like they were far outside what I could handle with my "natural abilities." I have never been more humbled or broken down. What's more, I felt almost zero passion or excitement for parenting during that first year. In fact, I often avoided home because it was so difficult and painful. Parenting was, and continues to be, the hardest thing I've ever done, as many parents realize. It feels like a magnifying glass on my weaknesses.

I'm often disappointed in my reaction or lack of patience, compassion, and empathy toward my kids. But every once in a while I have a moment when I surprise myself, either by what I'm willing to do for my children or by how much I truly love them.

Being a parent is far from easy or "natural." It's a learning curve for everyone. But it has been and continues to be a *transformational experience* for me, which has made not only me but my entire life better. And parenting is becoming an increasing passion and interest for me, something I want to do and be better at every single day. Something I know I can become great at.

It is often by taking opportunities or responsibilities above (or seemingly "unnatural" to) your skill level and experience that forces the greatest growth. If you're waiting to find something you feel immediate or intuitive passion for, then you're going to miss most of your greatest opportunities for growth and success. You'll miss countless opportunities to become more than you currently are. You'll fail to realize the truth that your personality, just like passion, is something you create based on what you put into life.

Waiting for a passionate opportunity to align with your innate personality is equivalent to saying, "There are millions of opportunities for growth out there. But I'm going to wait for the one in a million that exactly fits the narrow experience and perspective I currently have."

The "problem of discovery" also comes up in relationships. Because people have an idea of a fixed and innate personality, they spend loads of time looking for the "perfect" person to date and marry. Many people never commit to long-term relationships because of this fundamental misunderstanding about people. They think that when they find that "right" person, everything will just work out.

This is ignorance. Creating a successful marriage or partnership is just as difficult, and just as rewarding, as parenting.

Just as you will never "find" yourself, you will never "find" that perfect soul mate. The reason people want to find that perfect person, just like they want to find that perfect job, is because the "discovery" perspective is selfish. The end goal is all about meeting your own gratifications and happiness rather than happiness being the by-product of something much bigger. Of this, Harvard business professor Clayton Christensen said, "The path to happiness is about finding someone who you want to make happy, someone whose happiness is worth devoting yourself to."

Pro tip: *Don't marry for personality*. Why? Because personality will change over time. Obviously, there needs to be a connection. But the initial personality you fall in love with will not be the same person two, five, ten, or twenty years later. As the context and complexity of the relationship evolves—jobs, money, moving to new locations, kids, travel, aging, tragedies, successes, new information, new experiences, cultural shifts, identity shifts—each party's personality will change.

Moreover, even the most fascinating or attractive personality will lose its novelty over time. Rather than marrying a person for who they currently are, it takes far more wisdom and discernment to marry for who you can see them becoming—their future self—and how they will enable you to become your desired future self. Will marrying this person enable you to do and be all that you truly want? And will you enable them to be all that they truly want? Who and what could both of you become if you were partners?

Marry for aligned purpose, not personality. That purpose will transform both of you over time.

Developing a powerful relationship isn't about "finding," but *collaboratively creating and becoming* new people together, through the relationship. Both parties must adjust and change, becoming a more united whole that transcends the sum of the parts. If one or neither party changes for and through the relationship, then the relationship will be lopsided and will likely fail. High-quality relationships are transformational, not transactional. Often, the transformation is unpredictable and unexpected, as collaboration is a creative act.

So, what purpose are you creating for yourself?

What would happen if you stopped trying to find yourself, and instead became more creative and collaborative?

How would your personality develop and change if you went to work on it, chiseling and shaping it in desired ways?

Who would you be if you could creatively design yourself? (*Hint, hint: You can.*)

Myth # 5: Personality Is Your True and "Authentic" Self

The final myth is that your personality is your "authentic" self, which you should be "true" to. This myth leads people to being incredibly inflexible and narrow about how they view themselves.

Take, for example, the fact that many American teenagers are becoming increasingly inflexible. Many students across the country are demanding that they no longer be required to give in-class oral presentations, claiming their issues with anxiety make them "uncomfortable" with presenting in front of an audience. They believe they shouldn't be required to do something that feels so unnatural.

In an article published in the *Atlantic* entitled "Teens Are Protesting In-Class Presentations," one fifteen-year-old tweeted the following statement, which garnered more than 130,000 retweets and nearly half a million likes: "Stop forcing students to present in front of the class and give them a choice not to." Another teen tweeted,

"Teachers, please stop forcing students to present in front of the class & raise their hand in exchange for a good grade. Anxiety is real." Ula, a fourteen-year-old in eighth grade, reported, "Nobody should be forced to do something that makes them uncomfortable. Even though speaking in front of class is supposed to build your confidence and it's part of your schoolwork, I think if a student is really unsettled and anxious because of it you should probably make it something less stressful. School isn't something a student should fear."

Interestingly, many teachers agree with these students and are looking to provide alternative learning experiences that are less emotionally and socially risky, and instead more comfortable. Rather than helping the students become mature and confident, such teachers are catering to their demands, essentially validating a teenager's fixed mindset and lack of psychological flexibility.

A fundamental problem with traditional views of a fixed and innate personality is that people feel entitled to do only the things that feel natural or easy to them. If something is hard, difficult, or awkward, then people say, "I shouldn't have to do this."

It's instructive that "authenticity" is a highly prized value in modern society. People believe they have an "authentic" self—their "truth"—which is who they should be true to. This self is seen as innate, the "real" them. This line of thinking leads people to say things like, "I need to be true to myself. I shouldn't have to deny myself of how I'm feeling. I shouldn't have to lie to myself. I should be able to do what feels right to me."

Although well-meaning, this thinking reflects a fixed mindset, and often a reaction to trauma or a lack of healthy connection to parents. Often, kids from really extreme family situations—whether exceptionally strict or with practically zero guidelines—develop this desire for emotional-based self-direction.

I know many people who now, as maturing adults, are choosing limiting lives in the name of "authenticity" and being "real" with themselves. Pop culture has led people, like the eighth-grader mentioned above, to define "authenticity" as "however I feel right now." In digging deeper and asking questions, I often find that these people have feelings of inadequacy and fear falling short of the demands of their parents.

The desire to be "authentic" keeps people stuck in unhealthy patterns, trapped in their insecurities. Compare the complaining high school students to Wharton business professor and *New York Times* bestselling author Adam Grant, who explained how he got over his anxiety of public speaking. In order to become who he wanted to be, he had to give up his notions of his "authentic" self. At a commencement speech delivered at Utah State University, Grant said:

If authenticity is the value you prize most in life, there's a danger that you'll stunt your own development. When I was in grad school, a friend asked me to give a guest lecture for her class. I was terrified of public speaking, but I wanted to be helpful, so I agreed. I figured it would be a good learning opportunity, so after the class I handed out feedback forms asking how I could improve. It was brutal. One student wrote that I was so nervous I was causing the whole class to physically shake in their seats. My authentic self was not a fan of public speaking. But I started volunteering to give more guest lectures, knowing it was the only way to get better. I wasn't being true to myself, I was being true to the self I wanted to become.

"Authenticity" these days is usually another way of saying, "I have a fixed mindset. I am a certain way and shouldn't be expected to do anything but what comes immediately naturally and easy for me. I shouldn't have to do anything but what feels good, right now."

Your authentic self is not who you currently are, and it is definitely not who you used to be. Your authentic self is what you most believe in and who you aspire to be. Moreover, your authentic self is going to change. Being authentic is about being honest, and being honest is about facing the truth, not justifying your limitations because you don't want to be uncomfortable have hard conversations.

> Who do you really want to become?
>
> What would happen if you stopped trying to be "authentic," and instead faced the truth of why you're limiting yourself?
>
> What would happen if you had hard conversations with the important people in your life?
>
> What would happen if you were "true" to your future self, not your current fears?

Conclusion

Your personality is not something that can be captured by a simple personality test. Your personality isn't innate and unchanging. It's not your past, and it's definitely not the "real" and "authentic" you. It's not something you have to go out and discover so you can finally start living your life.

Although these perspectives are common, they are destructive myths that limit your potential and freedom as a person. If you've fallen prey to any of these cultural myths before, my invitation is for you to let them go, or at the very least question their validity and impact on your life and your future.

When you look at yourself or another person, you don't just see an unchanged "type." Instead, what you see is an identity, a story, a lot of history, expectations, culture, and so much more. People are dynamic. We should be more empathetic and understanding rather than judgmental and shallow.

As you will soon find, your personality is something you can decide and create for yourself. Personality is dynamic and malleable. When you understand how it works and the levers that move it, you become the director of who you become. You can radically advance in your life and success. You can become a better learner and be more flexible and adaptive. Your past and your future can increasingly become a story that you shape and define.

The rest of this book will show you how.

CHAPTER 2

The Truth of Personality

> Your vision of where or who you want to be is the greatest asset you have. Without having a goal it's difficult to score.
>
> —*Paul Arden*

After spending fourteen years in prison, Andre Norman went to Harvard and dedicated his life to helping other people. Although Andre's transformation has been amazing and unexpected, the reason he went to prison in the first place might be even more surprising.

Andre went to prison because he quit playing the trumpet at age fourteen.

Looking back on his life, Andre came to the realization that quitting the trumpet became his life's downward turning point, eventually leading him to quit everything else that mattered to him. Including himself.

"Bad people don't go to prison," Andre told my kids in our living room. "Quitters do."

Andre grew up in a ghetto of Boston. He was surrounded by other troubled kids in a corrosive environment with basically zero shot of "getting out." But by providence or luck, his sixth-grade teacher Mrs. Ellis saw potential in him. She was Andre's band teacher from sixth through eighth grade.

She helped him start playing the trumpet and showed a love and genuine interest in Andre that he'd never received before. Over time, Andre didn't want to let her down. He didn't do much in his other classes, but for Mrs. Ellis he showed up. He cared. Over a few years with Mrs. Ellis by his side, Andre began developing a talent for the trumpet.

That trumpet was the only thing in his life that gave him a healthy and creative outlet. His trumpet gave him a reason to go to school. It was, for a time, a defining characteristic of his identity. Something he was building his future hopes around. Something that gave him a sense of self and purpose.

When it was time for Andre to go to high school, Mrs. Ellis proactively filled out the paperwork for him to go to a magnet high school rather than the district high school where most of his classmates went. This magnet school had a great band program and her husband, Mr. Ellis, was the band teacher. She felt that Andre could be supported by her husband and that band could be a vehicle through high school, helping him bypass the numberless traps all around him.

Andre argued with Mrs. Ellis about the decision. But ultimately, she won the argument. He respected her because she stood up for him, even against the other teachers who saw nothing in him.

For ninth grade, Andre went to the magnet school. But he didn't exactly live out Mrs. Ellis's wishes and expectations. In explaining the situation to me, Andre told me he had two personalities at the time. On the one hand, he was a kid who loved music. On the other hand, he was a kid who wanted to be cool, not nerdy.

He viewed the other kids in his band class as nerdy. He didn't want to hang out with them despite loving band. He didn't really identify with them, and he didn't want to identify with them. Instead, he surrounded himself with what he perceived to be the "cool" kids, who also happened to be the troublemakers.

A few months into his first year, Andre's "cool" friends got sick of seeing him with his trumpet. "If you hang out with ten basketball players, then you shouldn't carry around a baseball," Andre told me. "They won't get it."

"Get rid of that stupid box or you can't hang out with us," they told him.

It was a hard decision, but Andre caved to the social pressure. He threw his trumpet into a dumpster, and along with it the side of him that loved music. Without his trumpet, he now only saw himself one way: as someone who was cool. From his perspective at that time, that meant replicating the juvenile and criminal behaviors of his friends. His trumpet, which had once represented his "purpose," was gone.

Without his purpose and the identity that went with it, Andre had no reason to continue going to school. It no longer fit with his identity or goals. He was no longer juggling two separate worlds, and instead jumped fully into the criminal behavior and persona of his social group. Over time, he began to see himself as someone who would hurt or kill to get what he wanted. And that's who he became.

By age eighteen, Andre was in prison for robbing drug dealers.

During the first six years inside, Andre became increasingly hostile to those around him. Prison is a dangerous environment, and Andre fully conformed. He quickly learned that there was a hierarchy in the gang world. Your rank in the hierarchy is based on the number and type of violent acts you do.

"You've got to win the mob, like in the movie *Gladiator*," he told me. "You need the crowd on your side. It's all about presentation and personality. You're only as good as your last fight."

Andre began rising the ranks within the prison gangs, becoming famous among that crowd. One day, he carried knives into the prison gym with the plan to kill eight specific people and then anyone else he didn't like. He knew he was going to get eight life sentences and so he thought, "Might as well add a few more on." His goal was to rise up the ranks of the hierarchy.

At the gym, he wound up stabbing several people.

"No one died, just a bunch of attempted murders," he told me, with some relief.

This act landed him in solitary confinement for two and a half years and added ten years to his prison sentence. But it also made him the number three guy in the hierarchy. And that's what his goal and focus was, so the extra years in prison and the confinement were badges of honor. Symbols of his growing status and fame. Solidification of the identity he was creating.

His goal shaped his identity, his identity shaped his actions, and his actions shaped who he was and was becoming. This is how personality is developed.

One day, toward the end of his time in solitary confinement, Andre was out on the recreational field for his daily hour of "rec" time. During this hour, a friend told him that some of his gang had been stabbed in another prison during a riot the night before.

This news made Andre angry, and he immediately began conceiving a plan in his mind about how he could kill those in his unit who were affiliated with the riot. "White guys stabbed my friends," he thought to himself, "so I'm going to kill all the white guys in my solitary confinement unit."

Andre's thinking was incredibly black-and-white, literally and figuratively. Because white people stabbed his friends, he saw that "white people" were to blame and had to be punished. "If Mexicans had stabbed my friends, I would have tried killing all the Mexicans," he told me. Andre's black-and-white thinking is reflective of traditional and common views of personality. We see people as types. We categorize them. We ignore nuance and context. We confirm our biases. We intentionally and subconsciously ignore what we don't want to see.

There were seven white guys in Andre's solitary confinement unit. All seven of them were also "ranked" gang members. Killing them would put Andre unquestionably at number one. This was his chance. His goals and vision were finally within reach.

"Once this guy stops talking, I'm going to go and kill those guys. Then I'll be the man," Andre thought to himself while listening to his friend recount the riot.

But before his friend stopped talking, something unexpected happened to Andre. It sunk in, on a more spiritual level, what the ultimate outcome of his actions and goals would be. The only way he can explain it is that he got a revelation from God. It was that profound.

God gave me my "Wizard of Oz" moment that day. At the end of *The Wizard of Oz*, Dorothy realizes there is no Wizard of Oz. It's all smoke and mirrors. It's all a hoax. Before that moment, I thought I was going to become the king of the world. Now I realized I was going to become the king of nowhere. This is nothing.

His storytelling friend noticed Andre spacing out. "Yo! What's going on, man? You listening to me?"

Andre was totally in his own head. It was dawning hard on him that trying to become the number one gang guy in prison was like chasing the Wizard of Oz. He'd been on the yellow brick road for the past six years. Once he made it to the end, there would be nothing there. It was all a hoax. A shallow pursuit.

So much of his life and identity were flashing before his eyes. On an emotional and spiritual level, he was finally questioning the validity of his current goals. He was considering the ultimate outcome, and whether that outcome—his future self and all that entailed— was something worth investing in and becoming.

This moment, when Andre truly questioned himself and his goals is fundamental to becoming a conscious human being. This is an experience you must have as well. Think for a moment about your own goals and ambitions.

What are you actually trying to accomplish in your life?

What is the ultimate end of what you're doing?

Why is *this* what you've chosen?

Is what you're doing worth it?

Are you on a yellow brick road to nowhere?

And even if you are headed "somewhere," are your sights too low?

Dr. Stephen Covey once said, "If the ladder is not leaning against the right wall, every step we take just gets us to the wrong place faster." The confidence you're seeking, and the power you know is within you, cannot be unlocked if you're pursuing the wrong goal.

What is at the end of your yellow brick road?

Where is your life going right now?

What wall is your ladder facing, and where will you be when you get to the "top"?

Andre didn't stab anyone that day. Instead, he walked back to his prison cell, sat on his bed, and thought to himself, "If I'm not going to be the king of nowhere, then what *am* I going to do?"

He had to rethink his entire life. His plan for the last several years was to be the king. Now being "the king" meant nothing. He needed a new goal.

Initially, he decided he wanted to get out of prison. He didn't want to be there anymore. But then he thought to himself that just "getting out" wasn't enough. Seventy-five percent of people who leave prison come right back. Lessons are repeated until they are learned. Instead of "being free," Andre made his goal to "be successful."

"Where do successful people come from?" he thought to himself. "They come from college. If I go to college too, then I'll be successful," was his reasoning.

Having grown up in Boston, he knew of only one school by name, Harvard. Sitting in his cell, rethinking his life and future after his Wizard of Oz moment, he decided he was going to go to Harvard.

Harvard become Andre's new trumpet.

It was a goal and purpose worth aspiring toward. Like his trumpet, he could construct a new identity around Harvard—an identity that would guide his behavior, friends, and choices. He became fixed on that goal. It became his purpose for being. It gave him something useful and constructive to think about, work toward, and build a new life around.

That single goal, his new purpose, gave Andre a path to getting out of prison and becoming a new version of himself. It ultimately shaped in him a new personality.

It took Andre eight more years to get out of prison. During those eight years, he got busy. Everything he did was filtered through and fueled by his new purpose. When the *why* is strong enough, you can get yourself through and do any *how*. Andre taught himself how to read and write, taught himself law, and learned anger management. An Orthodox rabbi become his mentor, helping him understand his life and how it had turned out the way it had. He came to understand forgiveness, responsibility, accountability, and service.

"The rabbi taught me how to be human," Andre told me.

Andre's new goal created a new lens, allowing him to see himself and his environment differently. He stopped noticing all the negative forces around him and began focusing on the opportunities for progress toward his goal.

After Andre got out of prison, he became the poster child for men who leave prison and change their lives. He became famous. He gave speeches all over the world, even at prestigious colleges like MIT and Harvard.

He became a fellow at Harvard in 2015, sixteen years after getting out of prison. He has his own office at the university. They've funded his projects to reduce riots and crime in the United States. Andre is now an internationally regarded public speaker. He's helped thousands of people overcome addictions and change their lives for the better.

Andre's story demonstrates *the truth of personality*. Andre's personality was shaped by his purpose. First his trumpet, then being the king, then Harvard. Each purpose shaped a different Andre.

Your personality is an effect, not a cause. The primary causes shaping your personality are your goals and the identity and behavior that flow from those goals. For most people, personality is a reaction to life events, circumstances, and social pressures. It isn't intentionally designed. It isn't questioned. It isn't chosen.

When you're intentional about where you're going, then you can become who you want to be. You can get off your yellow brick road. You can let go of who you've been. Your past doesn't need to be the ultimate predictor of who you are. Your behavior doesn't need to be consistent with who you've been. You can change. Radically so.

Let's break this down a little further.

Your Goals Shape Your Identity

Whether you realize it or not, everything you do has a purpose, or a goal, and these goals are what shape your identity. When Andre threw away his trumpet, continuing forward in band and becoming a musician ceased being his goal. As a result, he detached himself from that aspect of his identity. His purpose then became fitting in with his friends, which shaped his identity, actions, and circumstances. Over time, those things shaped his personality and future.

Your goals, not some predetermined set of fixed traits, shape your identity. Over time, and through repeated behavior, your identity becomes your personality.

An ancient concept in philosophy, known as *teleology* (from the ancient Greek *telos*, meaning "end goal"), can help us understand how this works. All human behavior *is fundamentally driven by, and is a function of, its end, purpose, or goal.* However, those goals may not be explicit or well defined. Jumping on YouTube to distract yourself for a few minutes has a purpose, even if it's just to distract yourself. Paying the bills. Hanging out with friends. Even engaging in hobbies and interests.

Even the most benign, unproductive behavior is goal-driven. Procrastinating and distracting yourself has a goal, even if that goal is to numb yourself for a while.

Every behavior has a reason. Realizing why you're engaging in a specific behavior is fundamental to becoming a conscious human being. Seeing every action you take as goal-driven allows you to take stock in the quality of your decision-making.

> Why are you engaging in this behavior?
>
> What is the purpose, reason, or end?
>
> What is the goal?
>
> How does this "goal" align with what you're ultimately trying to do?

Every behavior is ultimately driven by an outcome. That outcome may be spiritual, economic, urgent, social, or emotional.

If you asked Andre why he liked playing the trumpet, he might say it was fun, or because he liked his teacher, Mrs. Ellis. If you asked him why he wanted to fit in with the cool kids, he wouldn't have much explanation, except that he thought they were "cool" and wanted to be like them. Andre hadn't really examined his goals and their effect on his behavior. He wasn't conscious enough about where his desires or interests would take him.

As Socrates put it, "The unexamined life is not worth living."

Right now, we're going to take a second to examine your life. We'll start by examining what you've done in the past twenty-four hours, helping you see that *everything* you do is goal-driven. After that, we're going to dive into the three fundamental sources from which our goals come.

First, pull out a piece of paper and draw a line down the center. At the top of the left-hand side, write down "Activity." At the top of the right-hand side, write down "Reason."

Then list all of the activities you can remember doing in the past twenty-four hours. Everything you can fit on that page, at least. Here's an example of some of the things I've done in the past twenty-four hours and their associated reasons or goals.

ACTIVITY	REASON
Woke up at 5 a.m. to write	Book deadline
Listened to an audiobook	To take a break, get myself moving, and feel inspired
Ate lunch	Satisfy hunger and distract myself from work for a bit
Watched YouTube videos	Distract myself but also to see if LeBron James won
Worked out	Get my heart rate going
Went to Publix grocery store	Get juice for energy after workout
Talked to Draye	Get things organized for a launch we were planning
Recorded voice messages for an hour	Improve the launch
Wrote for a few more hours	Deadline was pending
Picked up Logan and Jordan from school	Support family and be with them
Went to Kaleb's baseball game	To support him

Now, each of these "reasons" likely has deeper reasons. For example, although my surface-level reason for going to the gym yesterday was to get my heart rate going, if you asked, "Well, why did you want your heart rate going?" I'd say, "So I can be healthy and focused." If you pressed and asked, "Well, why do you want to be healthy and focused?" I'd give yet another reason.

The point here is there is a reason for everything you did yesterday. Outcomes drove your behavior—outcomes you might not ultimately value. How you spend your time matters. It reflects your goals. It reflects the outcomes you're seeking for yourself. Looking at what you've done the past twenty-four hours and then examining the reason for your behaviors will help you see what your goals are.

Why did you do everything you did yesterday?

What outcomes were you seeking?

Are those the outcomes you really want? Or is your daily behavior a reflection of goals that were imposed upon you, either by society, circumstances, a traumatic experience, or something else?

You will only be able to control your time and yourself when you truly determine what you want for yourself. Your goals must be consciously chosen and then fiercely pursued. Spending your days on activities leading you to something incredibly important, something you truly value, is how you live without regret.

> Looking back at your list of activities from the past twenty-four hours, which ones are aligned with your future self?
>
> Which of those behaviors will your future self not engage in?
>
> Which of them, if removed, would free up more space and energy for what you ultimately want?

The Three Sources of All Goals

> Personal confidence comes from making progress toward
> goals that are far bigger than your present capabilities.
>
> —*Dan Sullivan*

All behavior is goal-driven. But where do "goals" come from? Fundamentally, goals come from three sources:

1. Exposure
2. Desire
3. Confidence

1. Exposure. Charlie Trotter was an American chef known for his influence on modern-day fine dining. For years, his Chicago restaurant was considered the finest and fanciest in America. Dishes were hundreds of dollars, served in a classy, elegant setting. And, regularly, Trotter would invite groups of impoverished children to eat at his restaurant for free.

He did this hoping to raise these kids' aspirations and goals. To expose them to a world completely different from the one they were conditioned to see.

He was opening their eyes.

Trotter received enormous criticism for giving underprivileged kids this rare and unique experience. "You'll make them unsatisfied and unhappy with their lives" and "You'll give them unrealistic expectations for what is possible" were the common complaints.

But Trotter didn't care what the critics said, because he would regularly receive mail from the children themselves, expressing immense gratitude for the experience and inspiration. Often, kids would say they wanted to become a professional chef when they grew up, or that they would grow up to create an even better restaurant than Trotter's.

Trotter was providing *subconscious-enhancing experiences* for these children. He was exposing them to a different way of living. He was providing an emotional experience within an enriched environment that opened the children's imaginations to new possibilities that they had never before considered.

You can't make decisions and choices if you don't know they exist. Your ability to make choices is limited by your context and knowledge. When you expand that context, you expand your options.

Your goals are based on what you've been exposed to. For instance, where I did my undergrad in psychology, the program's emphasis was counseling and social psychology. As a result, when I applied to graduate school the first time, I applied to counseling psychology programs, even though I wasn't sure those programs were the best fit for my ultimate aims.

A few months after getting rejected by all of the graduate schools I'd applied to, Lauren and I went on a three-week sightseeing trip to China. While there, I met a man who was a "Leader" at Apple for the entire Asian region. He told me his job involved training, motivating, and helping the leadership and teams at Apple be more effective.

As I listened to this man explain his job, it hit me square in the face. He was explaining exactly what I wanted to be doing.

"How did you get into this type of work?" I asked.

"I fell into it in kind of a weird way," he told me. "I actually have a law degree but navigated my way into this position. My boss has a master's in I/O psychology, though."

Interesting.

I remember vaguely hearing about I/O (industrial and organizational) psychology in an introductory psychology class for maybe five minutes. But otherwise, in my undergraduate program, I'd heard nothing about it. I did some googling and realized it was basically a perfect fit for what I was trying to learn and do.

My first time applying to graduate school, I was limited by what I knew. My second time applying, I had better information.

Those who become successful constantly expose themselves to new things. They travel, read books, meet new people. They prize education and learning. They seek to be surprised. They happily shatter their current paradigms for new and better ones—knowing that with better information, they can make more informed decisions. They can set better goals and aims for themselves. They can have better reasons.

Knowledge is key to setting goals. You can't pursue something you don't know exists. Exposure is the first source of goals. Whatever you're pursuing right now is based on what you've been exposed to. Creating better goals—and thus designing a better future—requires learning more, changing your perspective, and opening yourself up to something new. As General James Mattis, the twenty-sixth United States secretary of defense, put it, "If you haven't read hundreds of books, you are functionally illiterate and you will be incompetent because your personal experiences aren't broad enough to sustain you."

Read everything you can get your hands on. And then get better at filtering the best books from the rest. Reading biographies of inspiring people is one of the best ways to open up your mind to what you can do and become. Learn about the human condition, history, philosophy, psychology, spirituality, economics, and more. As you do, you'll change as a person. Your views will change. Your identity will change. Your goals will change.

Beyond reading books, you need to have experiences that stretch you, allowing you to see a different future, and giving you permission to actively pursue that future. Sometimes you need to go through very difficult experiences that show you that you can do hard things. Serving a mission did that for me, as did completing a PhD and becoming a father of five children in one calendar year. I've had many failures that have humbled me as well. Through all of these experiences, I've emerged a new person. Don't avoid experiences that will shape and transform you. Your future self must be stronger, wiser, and more capable than your current self. That can only happen through rigorous, challenging, and new experiences.

2. Desire. You won't pursue or engage in something if you don't want it. Statistics show that most people hate their jobs. Even still, they have their reasons for going to work—whether social, financial, or otherwise. Thus, they endure unenjoyable means to achieve their desired ends.

You spend your time engaging in activities because in the end, you believe those activities will get you what you want. But what if you want the wrong thing? Or, put another way, what if you *wanted something else*?

What if "paying the bills" was no longer the goal? Would you still keep that job you hated?

Just because you want something doesn't mean you should want it. Our desires do not come from our innate personality. Instead, our desires are trained, usually through experiences we've had, society, media, and those around us. Desires aren't innate. They are trained and fueled. They are clung to and identified with. Your desires shouldn't be mistaken as the "real" you. They are simply things you've attached meaning to, which you can also detach from or change the meaning of.

As an example, let's say you're a sports fan and have been since you were young. You may think being a sports fan is a part of your innate personality.

Not so.

Yes, sports are a part of your personality and identity. But you are the one actively fueling that side of your personality. You could stop fueling it. You could actively let go of that part of your identity and, over time, stop being interested in sports altogether. This may not be your goal or interest, but it is indeed possible. You'd need a reason to stop identifying with sports and continuing to carry that part of you into the future.

Just because you want something now doesn't mean you'll want it in five years or even next year. If you look back on what you wanted five years ago, chances are that much of what you wanted you no longer do. You've changed, your circumstances have changed, and thus your goals have changed.

Often, your current desires—such as sleeping in, binge-watching Netflix, or staying up late with friends—are at odds with better outcomes. Knowing that desires can be trained, and that your current desires were trained, allows you to question your current desires. It also allows you to proactively choose desires worth having and then training those desires to become genuine and deep.

You can get yourself to want anything. You might as well be intentional about what you train yourself to want.

If your future self is the evolved version of you, then your future self has a higher level of confidence, capability, and freedom than you presently have. They have different goals, concerns, and desires than you currently have.

Right now, you don't truly want what your future self wants.

Your future self is an *acquired taste.*

You have to *learn to want* and value what you don't currently want. If your future self is successful, you must learn to want what it takes to become successful. If your future self is healthier, you need to learn to want to be healthier. Training your desires is essential to choosing goals that are worth pursuing.

What you want right now may not truly be worth your time. I can speak for myself here: My current desires and directions may not be worth pursuing. I need to pause and question what I currently want. I know that my future self—the person I want to be—has knowledge, skills, characteristics, relationships, and more that I don't currently have.

Personality is all about preferences and interests. The "introvert" *prefers* sitting in the corner. But that same introvert can, if they wanted to, train themselves to prefer being in the crowd. But "being in the crowd" would have to be relevant to their ultimate goals. The "extrovert" may have trouble sitting alone in a room by themselves. But they can learn to do so, and quiet their minds, if they have a purpose.

When you evolve as a person, you develop a sense of purpose that expands beyond your personal preferences and interests. This purpose pushes you outside of your preferences, and ultimately shifts who you are.

You train desire by actively and intentionally pursuing it. As was discussed in the previous chapter, passion follows engagement and skills. You can learn to become passionate about anything. You might as well be intentional about what you choose to become passionate about. As Napoleon Hill stated, "Desire is the starting point of all achievement, not a hope, not a wish, but a keen pulsating desire which transcends everything."

Desire is the second source of goals. Your desires can and must be trained. Your life will become far more successful when you choose desires that produce outcomes your future self wants.

3. Confidence. You won't conjure or entertain goals you don't believe you can achieve. The list you wrote of your past twenty-four hours reflects your current level of confidence. Looking at your list, how many of those items required courage? How many came easily? How much of your time was spent advancing toward goals beyond your current capabilities?

Your job and income level are based on your confidence.

Your friends are based on your confidence.

How you dress is based on your confidence.

Confidence is the *basis* of imagination—which is required for seeing and choosing a future beyond your current capability and circumstances. Confidence reflects your personal belief in what you can do, learn, and accomplish.

The greater your confidence, the bigger your future self.

The challenge of confidence is that it can easily be shattered. Confidence is fragile, not constant. Traumatic and painful experiences can wreck your confidence and imagination. Every one of us goes through painful experiences that become an ever-present thorn in our side, paralyzing our ability, hope, and desire to move on.

The entire next chapter of this book focuses on trauma and its impact on personality. But for now, what you need to know is that trauma destroys your confidence. People often have very limited goals due to unresolved trauma. Sadly, when such is the case, then avoiding the painful emotions becomes the goal.

Confidence is built through acts of courage.

It takes courage to face the past, expose yourself to it until it no longer hurts, and change it. It takes courage to admit what you truly want with your life. It takes courage to attempt challenging goals, and to fail along the way.

While driving home from my office one day, I saw an extremely overweight man running in gym shorts and no shirt. His flabby body was glistening with sweat in the Florida sun.

This man inspired me. He was being audaciously *public* about his future self. He didn't care what I or anyone thought about his jiggling flab or stretch marks. His eyes were fixed on the steps ahead of him. His focus was laser. His sweat was dripping. His identity was shifting.

At some point or another, this runner became aware of and exposed to better ways of living. He saw value in improving his behavior and choices. He glimpsed himself as a healthier version of himself. He began to question his current desires. The quality and consistency of his behavior is based on the quality and specificity of his goal. If his goal is clear and compelling, he will be running a lot more and that fat will soon be gone. If his goal is not clear and compelling, then his running will be sporadic, inconsistent, and lead to mediocre results.

In any case, for at least that one moment, this man was acting from the perspective of a future self he hoped to become. He saw a different future for himself and had a reason to go out and run. If that purpose is fueled and his identity is trained, he could, and will, become that person.

Confidence is built through acts of courage and commitment. As he brazenly ran with an exposed and protruding belly, his confidence was skyrocketing.

This bold action was subconscious-enhancing. By courageously acting from the vantage point of your future self, you have peak experiences that enhance your subconscious, setting a new baseline for how you see yourself and the world, and a new baseline for what you expect. Peak experiences do not occur randomly but must be intentional. As the prolific writer and philosopher Colin Wilson explained:

> If you want a positive reaction (or a peak experience), your best chance of obtaining it is by putting yourself into an active, purposive frame of mind. . . . Depression . . . is the natural outcome of negative passivity. The peak experience is the outcome of an intentional attitude.

As you intentionally and courageously pursue meaningful goals, you'll have peak experiences. Those peak experiences will open you up, making you more flexible as a person. You will stop rigidly seeing yourself as the person you once were. You will become more confident and capable to create and achieve bigger goals.

Peak experiences are rare for most people, but can happen regularly. You could have a peak experience today if you choose to. You must be intentional. You must be courageous. You must move your life in the direction you genuinely want to go.

With each step this runner takes toward his future self, he believes more in its reality. His behavior reflects that reality, even if in the beginning that behavior is intermittent and inconsistent. Over time, if he continues acting consistent with his future, he'll want it more. His identity will become solidified. Eventually he'll get to the point where his future self is his current self, in all ways.

He'll no longer identify with his former self. He may no longer even remember what it was like to be his former self. The past will be informational, not emotional.

Confidence is key to the goals you set as a person. The greater your confidence, the more powerful your goals. Your confidence is something you must protect. You earn your confidence through intentional action toward meaningful goals. You can only borrow so much confidence from the distant past. More so, your confidence is based on who you've recently been.

You can build confidence through small but consistent actions reflecting your future self. You can also build confidence through daring and bold *power moves* toward your future self. A "power move" is an aggressive action toward your future self. It could be quitting a job you hate, investing in a mentor, going for a run in public, having an honest conversation, publishing a blog post even if you're scared, asking for a raise.

The more power moves you make, the more peak experiences you have. The more peak experiences you have, the more flexible and confident you'll become as a person. The more flexible and confident you are, the more imaginative and exciting will be the future you create and pursue.

Identity Should Be Intentionally Designed, Based on Your Desired Future Self

> Imagination is more important than knowledge. For knowledge is limited to all we now know and understand, while imagination embraces the entire world, and all there ever will be to know and understand.
>
> —*Albert Einstein*

Often, identity and personality are reactions to life events, circumstances, and habits. Few people intentionally define and shape their identity, based on who they plan to be, and then become *that* person. I say "that" person because your current and future selves are two different people.

Your future self *isn't* you. Your future self would do things differently, hopefully better, than how you do things now. Your future self should be evolved and different from your current self. To stay the same, although it is expected and even culturally celebrated, means you're not learning, advancing, and changing. Instead, you're stuck in a story, avoiding new experiences, and limiting your potential.

There's another reason why viewing your future self as a different person from your current self is essential for making big changes in your life. Without viewing yourself in an imagined and different way, it's actually not possible to engage in *deliberate* practice. This is called "deliberate" for a reason. You have a goal and the practice is targeted directly at that goal. The practice is purposeful and measured, not random and based merely on a "love of the process."

You need something—or better yet, *someone*—to be working toward. You need a vision that gives meaning and purpose to your practice. Yes, engaging in what you love for the sake of it is all well and good. But you won't actually push your perceived limits without visualizing your future self free of those limits.

Successful people start with a vision of their future self and use it as the filter for everything they do. Take, for example, Matthew McConaughey. During his speech after he won an Academy Award for Best Actor, McConaughey explained who his "hero" was:

> When I was fifteen years old, I had a very important person in my life come to me and say, "Who's your hero?" And I said . . . "You know who it is? It's me in ten years." So I turned twenty-five. Ten years later, that same person comes to me and says, "So, are you a hero?" And I was like, "Not even close! No, no, no." She said, "Why?" I said, "Because my hero's me at thirty-five." So you see, every day, every week, every month, and every year of my life, my hero's always ten years away. I'm never gonna be my hero. I'm not gonna attain that. I know I'm not, and that's just fine with me, because that keeps me with somebody to keep on chasing.

One day, you will become your future self. The question is: *Who is your future self?*

In answering this question, you should think in terms of what you'd ideally want. Not in terms of your current circumstances or identity. Who cares who you've been. Who do you want to be? That's your true and authentic self (for now).

Designing your future self requires imagining what their reality and daily experiences are like—the more vivid and detailed the better. What types of freedoms, choices, circumstances, experiences, and daily behaviors does your future self engage in?

When you become the architect of your own identity, you put less stock into how you view your current self. Your current self is important, but also limited. Your future self will be different. They'll see things differently. They'll have different freedoms. They'll have different relationships, daily activities, and experiences. What seems totally mind-blowing or exciting to you now is "normal life" for your future self.

Who do you want to be, if you were totally honest with yourself?

This is where you'll want to pull your journal out. Write down, in as much detail as you possibly can, who your future self is.

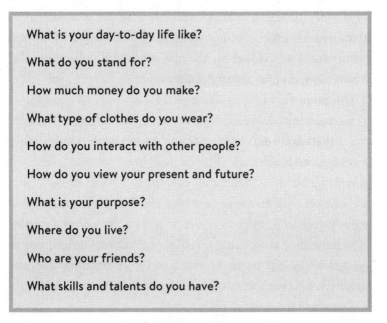

What is your day-to-day life like?

What do you stand for?

How much money do you make?

What type of clothes do you wear?

How do you interact with other people?

How do you view your present and future?

What is your purpose?

Where do you live?

Who are your friends?

What skills and talents do you have?

Select and Pursue One Major Goal: Your Future-Self Filter

> To decide on your mission, simply look over all of your goals and then ask yourself: Which one of these goals would enable me to become the person I need to be to achieve everything else I want in my life. The answer to that question is your mission.
>
> —*Hal Elrod*

After you've taken the time to really think about your future self, and about what their circumstances and possibilities are like, your next move is to think about the one major goal or outcome that would make your future self possible.

One goal.

Having multiple goals doesn't require that you focus. Having multiple goals is a reflection of fear and a lack of decision-making. You need *one major goal*. This one major goal needs to be measurable, definable, and visualizable. This one goal needs to clearly help and support all of the key areas of your life. This is why income goals are so powerful. If you're a writer, that goal may be a certain number of page views or subscribers. If you're a consultant, that goal may be the number of high-paying clients. If you're a runner, that goal may be the time of your marathon.

One goal creates focus.

Focus creates momentum.

Momentum and confidence spill over into all other areas of your life. That's why, in the book *The Power of Habit*, author Charles

Duhigg explains that when you improve one area of your life, all other areas improve as well. He calls this "keystone habits." Think of your one major goal as your "keystone goal." This one goal—by aggressively pursuing it and actively achieving it—helps you do *everything else* you're trying to do.

In the case of Andre, his one specific outcome was getting into Harvard. For him, that one outcome would allow him to become successful and not return to prison. Had Andre had five or more outcomes he was trying to pursue, he likely would never have gotten out of prison. His single goal gave direction and purpose to all of the sub-goals or other things he wanted to achieve.

Andre's single goal shaped his process for creating his future self. This is extremely important because, as of late, there is a lot of really bad advice when it comes to achieving success. Many people recommend focusing entirely on the "process," and essentially ignoring the result. Yet it's impossible to determine a "process," let alone an effective one, without a goal in mind. Moreover, without regularly measuring your progress and results along the way, it's impossible to determine if your process is working.

Your process must be based on the desired result you seek. You must begin with the end in mind. "Process" alone means nothing without the context of a goal. Process-first thinking is *tactical* and moves your life forward without a plan, trying to find whatever has worked for others.

Conversely, end-in-mind thinking is *strategic* and lived backward, where you reverse-engineer your process based on the results you want. Thus, "process" without measurement isn't a process at all. The desired outcome determines the process for getting it. The results you get along the way determine the adjustments to that process.

In his book *Zero to One*, billionaire Peter Thiel explains why "process" thinking leads to mediocrity. Instead, Thiel suggests having a "definite" attitude and purpose. As he states:

Indefinite attitudes to the future explain what's most dysfunctional in our world today. Process trumps substance: when people lack concrete plans to carry out, they use formal rules to assemble a portfolio of various options. This describes Americans today. In middle school, we're encouraged to start hoarding "extracurricular activities." In high school, ambitious students compete even harder to appear omnicompetent. By the time a student gets to college, he's spent a decade curating a bewilderingly diverse résumé to prepare for a completely unknowable future. Come what may, he's ready—for nothing in particular.

According to *expectancy theory*, one of the most researched and core theories of motivation, in order to have high levels of motivation, you need three things:

- A clear and compelling goal or outcome
- A path or process you believe will lead to the attainment of that goal
- A belief that you execute and succeed

You cannot have motivation without a goal. Research also shows you cannot have "hope" without a goal either. The more clear and definable the goal, the more direct the path and process. As you develop skills and knowledge, and move toward your goal, you'll develop the confidence that you can then execute and succeed. You'll want that goal more and more. Eventually, you'll get there and your whole life will be changed. You'll then have a new platform from which to set new and more stretching goals.

Commit to Your One Major Goal: Why Results Matter

> Commitment is a statement of what 'is'. You can know what you're committed to by your results, not by what you say your commitments are. We are all committed. We are all producing results. The result is proof of a commitment.
>
> —*Jim Dethmer, Diana Chapman, and Kaley Klemp*

Look at your life right now. Whatever you see, that's what you're committed to. Whatever you currently weigh, that's the weight you're committed to. However much money you make, that's how much money you're committed to making. Your commitment in life is reflected, 100 percent, by the results you're currently getting. If you were committed to something else, you'd have different results.

When you truly commit to the results you want, then your life starts improving. Your future self and the one major goal is what you should be committed to. Everything you do needs to be filtered through that one major goal.

The British rowing team—which hadn't won a gold medal since 1912—got committed in preparation for the 2000 Sydney Olympics. That commitment was embodied in a single question they asked themselves before making any decision: *Will it make the boat go faster?* This one question allowed them to measure every situation, decision, and obstacle—and to not get derailed from their objective.

With every decision or opportunity, every member of the team asked themselves: *Will it make the boat go faster?* If the answer was no, they didn't do it. They were committed.

Eat the donut? . . . (Will it make the boat go faster?)

Stay up late and go to the party? . . . (Will it make the boat go faster?)

Because they were committed, they got the result they wanted. They won gold that year.

In an a podcast, Lewis Howes interviewed John Assaraf, who shared what his first mentor taught him about goal-setting. After setting his goals in several areas of his life (e.g., health, spirituality, finances, relationships, service, etc.), and for one, three, five, and twenty-five years out, Assaraf's mentor asked him, "Are you interested in achieving these goals, or are you committed?" to which Assaraf responded, "What's the difference?" His mentor responded: "If you're interested, you come up with stories, excuses, reasons, and circumstances about why you can't or why you won't. If you're committed, those go out the window. You just do whatever it takes."

You get whatever results you're committed to. But, as a culture, we've been brainwashed to shy away from committing to *specific* outcomes. We've been taught that if we overcommit to something, then we'll set ourselves up for failure and letdown. We've been taught that we should ignore the outcome and focus exclusively on the "process" instead. Committing to a specific result feels too scary, or too obsessed with externalities.

However, there are several benefits to committing to specific results. For example, when you commit to something specific, you're forced to be honest with yourself and with everyone else about what you truly want. Being honest is rare. Most people hold their true desires tight to their chest. They are afraid to fully admit what they want most in life. But when you commit to a specific outcome, you've got to make that outcome your new narrative. That's what you're going to do. You may not know exactly how it will all play out, but you're going to get there. That level of honesty and transparency is both rare and contagious—evoking confidence as you begin making progress, and conjuring desire to support as well as help from others.

Another reason to commit to specific results is that it clarifies your identity. Your identity comes from your goals. Being totally bought-in and clear about the end you have in mind instills a deep sense of purpose. You can imagine your future self in the position you want to be. Without a clear outcome, your identity becomes muddled. Who are you really? What are you really all about? What are you going to do? Who are you going to be?

Committing to a specific outcome—your one major goal—also forces you to improve. For example, when I started blogging online, I noticed that other writers, those committed to their process, would publish tons and tons of articles. But they weren't getting any better. As the years passed by, I went on to become a professional writer. Many of those bloggers are still banging away, blog post after blog post. But their results haven't changed because they haven't committed to a clear outcome.

When you commit to a specific outcome, you're forced to get better. Your results speak for themselves. If your results aren't getting better, then you should question how interested or committed you are to this thing. You'll know you're serious about improving your results when you really begin tracking everything you do, down to the minutest detail. As Pearson's Law states, "When performance is measured, performance improves. When performance is measured and reported, the rate of improvement accelerates."

Committing to specific results also enhances motivation. According to *expectancy theory*, you cannot be motivated without a goal. The more singular and focused your goal, the more direct the path. The more direct and clear the path, the more motivated you will be. Complexity kills motivation, which is why lasering in on one keystone goal changes the game. A single goal allows for a more streamlined path, which allows you to not only see the outcome but also the path to making that outcome real. This skyrockets motivation and confidence.

Finally, committing to a specific result increases your faith. Napoleon Hill stated that "A definite purpose, backed by absolute faith, is a form of wisdom and wisdom in action produces positive results." It doesn't take much faith to say, "I'll try," or "We'll see what happens." But it does take intense faith to say, "This will happen. I don't exactly know how, but it will happen." This level of commitment forces you to your knees with greater sincerity. It leads you to doing things you'd never otherwise do. It forces miracles to occur.

Are you willing to commit to your future self?

Are you willing to commit to one specific goal?

Are you willing to put it all out on the line?

Are you willing to be honest about what you truly want?

Are you willing to refine and enhance your process to ensure improved results?

Go to Bed One Hour Earlier: Eliminate Destructive Consumption

> A mistake repeated more than once is a decision.
>
> —*Paulo Coelho*

When you commit to a bigger future, you're forced to improve how you spend your evenings and mornings. The end of the day is a time for relaxation and reflection, not unhealthy consumption. By the end of the day, you've made a lot of decisions and are exhausted. As a result, your willpower is all dried up. Low willpower leads to high and unhealthy consumption behaviors—mostly the seeking of quick-release dopamine.

Social media, sugar, carbs, and other distractions are common evening activities for many people. With low willpower, it's easy to fall into bad choices. These choices provide a short dose of dopamine or distraction, but come with a heavy cost. Engaging in wasteful and unhealthy behaviors at night negatively impacts your sleep, sets up your next morning for failure, and robs you of your confidence.

Watching a movie and spending quality time with loved one's is different from spacing out on your smartphone with your family wanting your attention.

If you're committed to becoming your desired future self, you need to avoid the pitfalls that come from low willpower at night. Otherwise, you're taking one step forward during the day and stepping backward at night. This slows your progress.

Success at night and in the morning is crucial to becoming your future self.

A powerful antidote to wasteful distractions and poor behaviors at night is to go to bed sooner. Rarely are the evening hours spent powerfully. Usually, there is a point of diminishing returns—usually after eight or nine p.m., give or take an hour. Unless you're doing something that connects you to your loved ones, you're better off getting yourself to sleep earlier. Going to bed one hour earlier than your norm is one of the fastest ways to becoming your future self. You avoid wasteful consumption. You get more rest. You enable yourself to wake up earlier and get to work on your goals before the busyness of the day takes hold.

Most people go to bed far later than they should due to cultural norms. Going to bed after ten is unlikely to help you become your future self. You may be seen as a weirdo for going to bed progressively earlier. But not for long. Over time, your results will speak for itself. You'll be getting more and better rest. You'll be waking up earlier and with more confidence because you are avoiding goal-conflicting consumption.

Mark Wahlberg, as an example, goes to bed at seven p.m. so he can wake up at three a.m. to train his body at the elite level that allows him to do the work he does. He's clear on his goals. His future self is much bigger than most people's. Therefore, he's willing to engage in a process, routine, and schedule that most people view as extreme or strange.

Go to bed one hour earlier. Avoid the nighttime hours when your willpower and decision-making ability are lowest. Set yourself up for success the next morning.

Wake Up One Hour Earlier: Make Power Moves Daily Toward Your Future Self

> Lose an hour in the morning, and you will spend all day looking for it.
>
> —*Richard Whately*

Get up early and start getting after your future self.

If you wake up early and immediately begin making power moves toward your dreams, you'll build confidence and momentum that will ripple through the rest of your day. You'll make better decisions and come off as far more congruent to those around you. As a result, you'll start having better twenty-four-hour periods.

If you improve your days, you'll improve your life. If you wait to wake up until you have to, and thus only engage in "urgent" activities, then you won't make meaningful progress in your life. You'll maintain the status quo, and, as a result, your time will fly by. The days, weeks, and years will pass you by and you won't make meaningful progress.

If you're going to achieve your one major goal and become your desired future self, then you need to be courageous. You need to take bold steps in the direction of your goal, daily.

Any bold move toward your goal is a power move. Power moves are subconscious-enhancing, resetting what is "normal" behavior for you. By engaging in intentional, goal-directed behavior in the morning, you'll begin having peak experiences on a daily basis. Your brain and identity will change. Your confidence will increase. Your identity will become more flexible, allowing you to detach from who you've been and become your desired future self.

Peak experiences increase flexibility and confidence. Peak experiences require intentionality and proactive action. By going to bed with a purpose, waking up, and immediately making progress toward your future self, peak experiences will become commonplace for you. You'll begin learning a ton each day, and with learning comes change. As the British philosopher Alain de Botton said, "Anyone who isn't embarrassed by who they were twelve months ago isn't learning enough."

According to Abraham Maslow, the psychologist who coined the term and framework for self-actualization, having these types of stretching experiences—what Maslow called "peak experiences"—is how you become self-actualized. In fact, such experiences are required to get to that level.

Self-actualization is the idea that you are no longer inhibited by internal or external limitations but are free to pursue your highest potential and aims. Maslow defined peak experiences this way: "Rare, exciting, oceanic, deeply moving, exhilarating, elevating experiences that generate an advanced form of perceiving reality, and are even mystic and magical in their effect upon the experimenter."

Peak experiences are rare because few people are proactively and intentionally creating a future self. Few people are committed to a specific future. Few people are courageously making power moves on a daily basis.

My questions for you are:

Are you going to create more peak experiences?

Are you going to be more active and intentional with your time?

Are you going to exercise more courage and commitment?

Are you going to act toward your future self, become more flexible, and stop insisting that your former self is who you really are?

In order to become more flexible and facilitate regular peak experiences in your life, you'll need to embrace *uncertainty*. As Harvard psychologist Dr. Ellen Langer explains, "If there are meaningful choices, there is uncertainty. If there is no choice, there is no uncertainty." If you're unwilling to face and interact with uncertainty, then you've greatly limited who you are and what you've become. You've limited your ability to make choices, because all choices involve uncertainty and risk.

Uncertainty can be difficult to handle. According to Dr. Daphna Shohamy, a neuroscientist at Columbia University's Zuckerman Institute, a primary purpose of our brain is to *predict* the outcomes of our behavior.

That's the most important utility of the brain. It's why we form memories—to be able to accurately predict the future. The ability to predict the future and plan is what has allowed humans to thrive as a species for thousands of years.

What does this mean on a personal level?

Your brain is designed to *keep you outside of situations of uncer-*

tainty. Uncertainty is something to be avoided. For this reason, when you're in a new situation or trying something you've never done before, you often get a rush of emotions, like anxiety or fear. Several researchers argue that the unknown is in actuality the foundation of all fears. The fight-or-flight response is a chemical signal from your brain that you have no clue what might happen, so you had better get back to safety.

Your brain wants your life to be safe and predictable. Your brain will try to stop you from putting yourself in risky situations. However, paradoxically, your brain formulates its most powerful memories and learning as you experience new things—especially when your predictions about the future are wrong!

Dr. Shohamy explains that our brain changes and learns through "prediction errors," which occur as we incorrectly predict what will happen. A *prediction error* is another term for failing. *Failing* is another term for learning. And *learning* is another term for changing.

Your future self will see the world differently than your current self to the degree that you learn and change. If you want to accelerate your learning, you'll need to embrace uncertainty. You'll need to take risks and make mistakes. As you do, you'll experience far more emotions—highs and lows—and through those experiences you'll change as a person. Those are the very peak experiences you can have daily when you become fully committed to your future self, instead of your current or former self.

Life becomes a lot more exciting and less repetitive when your future self becomes your daily mission, rather than avoiding uncertainty and change. Avoid consumption at night. Create peak experiences in the morning.

Transform Yourself Daily
Through Journaling

> Only through imaging a future self with improved skills may
> we be able to motivate, plan, and execute the honing of skills
> through deliberate practice.
> —*Dr. Thomas Suddendorf, Dr. Melissa Brinums, and Dr. Kana Imuta*

Your journal is a brilliant place to actively convince yourself, emotionally, that what you want is already yours—you influence yourself through strategic communication.

Many people think "journaling" is about documenting the past. It can be. But envisioning and strategizing the future will internalize and clarify your goal.

It is important to note, though, that in order to effectively influence or persuade yourself during your daily journaling sessions, you want to set the stage internally and externally before you start writing. With the right preframe ritual, your journaling sessions will become daily peak experiences, putting you into a peak state from which to live out the rest of your day. You can preframe yourself for peak experiences in the following ways:

* Getting yourself into a distraction-free environment where you can think freely and without notifications going off (leave your smartphone either away from your body or on airplane mode)
* Meditating or praying before writing
* Reviewing your vision or goals before writing
* Writing about things you're grateful for—past, present, and future

Although it doesn't matter what time of day you journal, just before or just after sleep are optimal, as your subconscious is most susceptible to influence due to the slowed state of your brain waves during these times. When writing, be mindful of your environment and how it is influencing your thoughts and emotions. Ideally, you would have a designated space for journaling, visualization, and future-pacing.

Once in your creation-space environment, take some deep breaths, and meditate or pray for a few moments before opening your journal. Affirm that you're going to be successful today. That you're going to succeed in what you're trying to accomplish. That life is amazing.

Open your journal slowly.

Before you begin writing, review your goals. This includes your one major goal and a subset of smaller, more short-term goals. They should be written somewhere easily accessible. Reviewing your goals before writing in your journal activates the mindset and circumstances of your future self, so that when you begin writing in your journal, *you're writing as your future self, from their vantage point and perspective.*

My own goals are written on the inside cover of my journal, so that every time I open it, all I need to do is look at that inside cover. Every month or so, I go through an entire journal and thus reassess and rewrite these goals. My goals are framed by answering the following questions:

- Where am I now?
- What were the wins from the past ninety days?
- What are the wins I want from the next ninety days?
- Where do I want to be in three years?
- Where do I want to be in one year?

Every time I open my journal, I start by looking at the front cover and reading my answers to these questions. Of course, my answers—even my goals—change even on a monthly basis. It's totally fine and expected that your plans adjust over time.

By looking at the recent wins from my last ninety days, I immediately feel a sense of movement and momentum. This gives me confidence. By seeing what I'm trying to accomplish in the short and long term, *I'm reminded of my future self.*

Each of these activities—from getting into the right environment, meditation, breathing, and viewing your recent wins and goals—puts you into the right mindset, so that when you write, you write from a higher and more powerful place.

There's one more crucial thing you'll want to do to properly get yourself in the right mindset, and that's starting your writing from a place of gratitude and abundance.

The effects of gratitude journaling are well documented. Research has shown that gratitude consistently improves people's emotional well-being. The regular practice of writing and reframing through gratitude can transform depression, addiction, and suicidal thoughts. Gratitude has been found to heal and transform relationships. In almost every way imaginable, gratitude has been found to help.

Up until recently, most of the research on gratitude has been self-reported. New studies, however, are showing that gratitude journaling not only affects emotional well-being, but can also improve the biomarkers of legitimate health risks such as heart failure.

Cardiac patients who are in Stage B, otherwise known as pre-heart failure, have a small window of time for reversing the downhill spiral toward fatal heart failure. In one study, doctors decided to have their patients try gratitude journaling during this small window. Patients were randomly assigned to either the experimental group or the control group. Those in the experimental group did an eight-week gratitude journaling intervention. Those in the control group underwent "treatment as usual" without gratitude.

After the eight weeks, all of the patients from both groups underwent assessments that included a six-item gratitude questionnaire, resting heart rate variability, and an inflammatory biomarker index. Those who practiced gratitude journaling showed a drop in heart failure symptoms and had reduced inflammation.

Praying about, meditating on, and then writing what you're grateful for at the beginning of your journaling session immediately shifts your emotional and physical state, as well as your perspective. Gratitude and excitement, as well as confidence, can become the lens through which you write about both your past experiences and your future ones. When writing through the energy of gratitude, you'll have positive expectations without unhealthy attachment toward what you're trying to accomplish.

You'll write from a place of joy, peace, and bliss. This emotional state will bring about lots of ideas you can execute, which will likely also take courage to accomplish. These are the exact emotions that will upgrade your subconscious and ultimately create your future self and circumstances.

Then, just write.

Don't get overly attached to what you write about. You are only writing for your own psychological benefit. No one else will read this. Just write about your goals. They could be in bullet points. They could be in pictures. There's no right or wrong way to do it.

Write with the expectation and excitement that your future self is real, and that you will be successful. Think in terms of what needs to be done to move yourself forward. Write down all of the things you'll need to do now and people you'll need to reach out to.

Expect to Succeed: A Conversation with Your Future Self

In December of 2019, Joe Burrow, the college quarterback for Louisiana State University (LSU), won the Heisman Trophy, the highest individual award for an outstanding player in NCAA football. Interestingly, two years earlier, Burrow had to make a difficult decision. He was the backup quarterback for Ohio State, and unless he made a switch, he wouldn't be able to fully attempt his dreams.

So he transferred to LSU. During the 2018 season, Burrow and the LSU Tigers went 10–3. That season he threw 2,894 yards with 16 touchdown passes and had 5 interceptions. He showed signs of being a good quarterback, but nobody expected what would happen during the 2019 season. In 2019, LSU went undefeated, broke several single-season records for any college football team in history, and won the national championship. Burrow shattered several records himself, throwing 5,671 yards with 55 touchdowns and 6 interceptions.

In one season, Burrow went from being a pretty good quarterback to having arguably the greatest single season for a college quarterback in history. By the end of the 2019 season, he was the number one projected draft pick for the NFL's 2020 season and the Heisman Trophy winner.

Nobody saw this coming, except Burrow.

In an interview with ESPN following the Heisman Trophy award, Burrow was asked: "Joe, if I had told you two seasons ago that you were going to win the starting job, you were going to beat Alabama, you were going to win a Heisman, you were going to be in the playoffs, you would have said what to me?"

Burrow's response was inspiring and important. He replied:

> *I would have believed you.* [emphasis mine] I know the work I'd put in up to that point. I just felt like I needed an opportunity. I knew the kind of players that were here, and Coach O sold me on a vision. I knew the work we had put in this offseason. So we totally expected to be in this position.

In 2017, Burrown had no evidence of the outcome. The fact is, what happened was so monumental that he should *not* have believed it was possible. But he did.

And that's why it did happen.

Thinking about yourself, what would happen if your future self came to you and told you that everything you want to see happen was going to happen? Would you believe them? The answer better be yes. Because unless you believe it, it's not going to happen. You need to be fully committed to becoming your future self and all that involves. That commitment will lead you down a crazy path. You'll need to make hard decisions and follow your gut, sometimes against the advice of well-meaning people.

If your future self came to you and told you of the monumental things that happened, would you believe them?

Conclusion

The truth about personality is that it can, should, and does change. Your goals shape your identity. Your identity shapes your actions. And your actions shape who you are and who you're becoming. This is how personality is developed.

The next several chapters focus specifically on the core levers of personality, those things you can directly control and that indirectly shape who you become. Every time you reimagine a future self and seek to achieve stretching goals, you'll need to change each of these "personality levers."

These four levers are:

- **Trauma**, which either traps you in the past or propels extreme transformation and growth
- **Identity narrative**, which is the story you tell about yourself and can be based either on your past or your desired future
- **Your subconscious**, which pulls you back to homeostasis but can be continually upgraded through emotional experiences and future-self behaviors
- **Your environment**, which either sustains who you are or forces you to evolve into someone new

Unless you're strategic, these four levers will keep you locked in repetitive and predictable cycles. You'll feel stuck and change will feel hard, if not impossible. However, when you understand how to move and shift these levers, then changes to your personality become sudden, dramatic, and inevitable.

The next four chapters will take on each of these four levers, one by one, teaching you how to use them effectively. As you do, you'll be enabled to experience self-directed and radical transformation in your life and as a person.

> Give me a lever long enough and a fulcrum on which to place it, and I shall move the world.
>
> —*Archimedes*

CHAPTER 3

Transform Your Trauma

> Being traumatized means continuing to organize your
> life as if the trauma were still going on—unchanged and
> immutable—as every new encounter or event is
> contaminated by the past.
>
> —*Bessel van der Kolk*

Rosalie is a kind and lovely woman in her eighties who never fulfilled her dream of writing children's books. Not because she had a hard life or couldn't read or grew up in extreme poverty and needed to feed herself. She never wrote children's books because, over fifty years ago, someone unintentionally made her feel bad.

I met Rosalie at a conference. During the few days we were together, I noticed her scribbling short stories and poems. When I asked her about it, I learned that she had always wanted to write and illustrate children's books. When I asked her why she hadn't created any books, she said she wasn't good at drawing.

Surprised, I asked what she meant. She then went on to detail an event that occurred over fifty years prior.

Back in the late 1960s, while she was raising her young and growing family, Rosalie decided to start taking art classes. For as long as she could remember, she had wanted to write, illustrate, and publish children's books.

One night during an art class with a handful of other people, Rosalie had an experience that ended her dream. After a particular drawing exercise, the teacher went around the room checking each student's work. When he stopped at Rosalie, he grabbed her chalk and "corrected" her drawing.

During the sixty or so seconds that the teacher was drawing over her work, Rosalie felt extremely embarrassed. None of the other students had been corrected in this manner. All eyes were on her. This was all too painful for her to handle. In the emotional swirl of the moment, a thought entered her mind: *I must not be very good at this.*

Rosalie never attempted drawing again.

As I listened to her recount this experience, my jaw was on the floor. She was narrating this incident from fifty years ago as if it had happened just last week.

"So, wait . . ." I said, stumbling over my words. "After all these years, you've *never* tried illustrating your children's stories?"

"No," she replied. "I don't have the native ability to draw."

There was no emotion. From her perspective, she was stating cold facts. Reality. There was no convincing her. I tried on multiple counts during the few days we were together.

"If you had the ability to draw pictures, would you create children's books?" I asked.

"It would be a lot of fun," she replied.

Over the years, the thought to write and illustrate children's books occasionally popped into her head. But almost immediately, that terrible art class experience and how she felt would come to her mind. The pain of that moment would be reignited and her imagination would immediately blank out. All the reasons why "now" isn't the right time would pop up. This is what Steven Pressfield called the "Resistance"—a universal force that stops people from engaging in creative acts.

This resistance, born of trauma, is why before entertaining the idea or taking any action, *Rosalie would stop herself.*

The saddest part is that she *still* wishes she could illustrate children's books but honestly believes she can't.

When most people think of "trauma," they imagine it only in its extreme manifestations, such as a diagnosed disorder like PTSD. Trauma is not limited to major, easily recognized events, though. Trauma, in a variety of forms, is part of each of our lives. It includes any negative experience or incident that shapes who you are and how you operate in the world. We have all experienced and have been, or are, impacted by trauma.

In this chapter, you'll learn how trauma can and does shape personality. In fact, you'll learn that rather than building the life we genuinely want, far too often we build our lives *around our trauma*. To avoid the pain of the past, we create a pseudo-personality rather than our desired one.

After learning how trauma shapes our lives and goals, you'll learn how to process, frame, and overcome your trauma so your past doesn't limit your future.

Trauma Shatters Hope and Eliminates the Future

Dr. Jennifer Ruef is a professor of mathematics education. She has been training teachers on better ways to teach math for the past thirty years in the hopes of helping children realize they *can* indeed learn math. This is no easy task, and in fact is one of the biggest challenges US math educators face, because so many students suffer from "math trauma"—a form of debilitating mental shutdown when facing mathematics.

Math teachers, particularly in junior high and high school, have a really hard job. Most of their students genuinely believe they aren't good at math and therefore give minimal effort or attention. At some point in a given student's life, they had a bad experience with math that they internalized as an identity narrative—*I'm not good at this. I don't like this.*

Math trauma manifests as anxiety or dread, and an incapacitating fear of being wrong, according to Dr. Ruef. Tragically, this fear limits options such as school and desired career choices for many people— not because they *couldn't* do math but because trauma-induced fear paralyzed them.

Sometimes a student may perform well on initial tests and assignments but still fear making mistakes or revealing weakness or incompetence to a teacher or parent. Those who shy away from challenging work, making mistakes, or revealing incompetence have what Dr. Ruef refers to as a "fragile math identity." They are keeping up an appearance that, like thin glass, can be shattered with the slightest negative emotional experience. They *avoid* rather than pursue failure, and as such, the inevitable eventually occurs when they reach their skill cap and "fail." For those avoiding failure, reaching their skill cap can be traumatic.

According to Dr. Ruef, the most common experiences leading to math trauma are being told you aren't good at math by an adult, panicking over timed math tests, or getting stuck on some math topic and struggling to move past it. Without the help of a support-ive teacher, mentor, or parent, the student gives up.

I can't do this.

Pain and failure become associated with math. All imagination and interest toward math fades. A "future" involving math no longer becomes an option.

That's the spirit of trauma. A hallmark of trauma is that it stops you from being psychologically flexible. Instead, you become rigid and fixed in your thinking. Hence, research has shown that individuals suffering from PTSD often score zero on imagination. Imagination is all about mental flexibility—seeing and believing different angles and possibilities.

When traumatized, you start thinking in black and white. Instead of seeing different perspectives and contexts, you focus exclusively on the *content* of what occurred.

I failed the test. I'm not good at this.

You believe your viewpoint is objective rather than just a single and limited perspective of an event or experience. This type of thinking creates what Stanford psychologist Carol Dweck calls a "fixed mindset," which is the belief that you cannot change, grow, or develop in specific areas. It is the belief that your skills, personality, and character are "fixed" traits that are innate and unchangeable.

According to Dweck, the fixed mindset is an approach to life *defined by the past*. The opposite of a fixed mindset is what Dweck calls a "growth mindset," which is the belief that you can change your traits and character. Having a growth mindset means your life is *defined by the future* and focused on what can change.

Because Rosalie defined herself by her negative interpretation and attachment to the art class experience all those decades ago, she has a fixed mindset about herself. As a result, she focuses on what she believes to be her "natural" or "innate" traits. In her mind, given her lack of art "genes" or "traits," it is impossible for her to become a good artist.

Having a fixed mindset is a "premature cognitive commitment." As various psychologists have explained, premature cognitive commitments occur without critically evaluating what happened. The commitment is emotionally based with little depth of evidence to support or justify it.

When people have a traumatic experience—even a small one— the emotions of the moment are enough to justify a new cognitive commitment.

I can't do this.

I'm not worthy.

I'll never have the life I want.

I should stay away from this.

In the case of Rosalie, she committed mentally to the idea that she isn't good at art and therefore shouldn't do it anymore: *I don't have the native ability to draw.* This commitment was forged during a terrible emotional experience. She never questioned the validity or value of that commitment. Instead, she buried it and never spoke about it for years.

Research on both trauma and the fixed mindset shows that they each individually lead to an *exaggerated fear of failure.* The greatest fear of the fixed mindset, according to Dr. Dweck, is fully attempting something with everything you've got and still coming up short. If such were to occur, then you'd have to accept that you simply don't have what it takes and should do something else.

People don't want to deal with that kind of failure. It would make too big a mark on their identity, leaving them feeling like a total and utter failure. Instead of even trying, they convince themselves to simply go for something else—something less risky and more certain.

As the author Robert Brault said, "We are kept from our goal not by obstacles but by a clear path to a lesser goal."

It is not the obstacles between ourselves and our dreams that stop us. Rather, we are stopped by our commitment to the idea—to the identity—that we can never actually achieve our goals. That we don't have what it takes. Instead of committing to what we truly want, we commit our time and attention to lesser goals.

We settle for a lesser future self. Our imagination, faith, and confidence to conjure and pursue a more exciting and powerful future self aren't there. We become increasingly rigid about who we are and what we're capable of. The past defines and drives our lives.

This is why making commitments about ourselves and our future should not be done while we're in a traumatic or emotionally broken state. From that state, our decisions for ourselves and our future will be limited. Instead, we want to make our decisions and commitments while in a peak and heightened state—when our faith and expectations are high.

Some psychologists might argue that Rosalie made the right decision to abandon her dream of creating children's books. Rather than disappointing herself with delusional goals, she was realistic. She didn't have the skills or capacity to become a great cartoonist or illustrator. Thus it was better for her to be true to her "authentic" self.

This kind of thinking suggests we should build our life and goals to match our innate personality and talents. If you're a square peg, then stop trying to fit yourself through round holes—even if those round holes are the opportunities or future you genuinely want for yourself.

It's not surprising, then, that personality is often the by-product of trauma. As trauma expert Gabor Maté, MD, says, "What we call the personality is often a jumble of genuine traits and adopted coping styles that do not reflect our true self at all but the loss of it."

> **Quick exercise:** Describe one negative or traumatic experience that you've had in your past. In what ways has this experience led you to pursue "lesser goals" or held you back in your progress in any way?
>
> Now reframe those negative experiences by writing how they could ultimately help you become a stronger person.

Personality as the By-Product of Trauma

On my daughter's tenth birthday, our son Logan came to my wife with a sliver of glass stuck in the heel of his foot. Lauren got the tweezers and Logan panicked. She told him to leave the glass in as long as he wanted and come back when he was ready to have it taken out.

He left relieved to have avoided the dreaded tweezers and tried enjoying the party. But with the glass in his heel, he couldn't run. The other kids were running around and playing. Even getting in the pool was too risky. He had to walk on the outside edges of his feet awkwardly, slowly, and painfully.

He wanted to play.

He returned, humbled and reluctant, to have the glass removed.

It was a painful twenty seconds, but afterward, Logan was able to get on with the party.

This event reminded me of Michael Singer's book *The Untethered Soul,* in which he describes a person who is accidentally pierced in her arm by a large thorn, causing electrifying pain with the slightest brush. She leaves the thorn in her arm, instead of going through the pain of taking it out.

Yes, she avoids the intense pain of removing it, but there is a cost to this decision: In order for her to live with the thorn in her arm, she must ensure that *nothing touches* the thorn.

She is no longer able to sleep on her bed, because there is a chance she can roll over and touch the thorn while asleep. To cope, she creates a device to sleep in that ensures her thorn remains untouched.

She loves playing sports, but she fears that the physical activity of sporting may hit the thorn and cause excruciating pain. So she develops a pad to wear that protects her arm from contact. Although this pad is uncomfortable and limits her ability to perform well, at least she can play the sports she loves while also protecting her thorn.

This woman ultimately alters every area of her life to ensure that nothing touches her thorn. From her work to recreation to relationships, she's constructed a new life and environment to free herself from the troubles of her thorn.

Or has she?

Rather than creating the life she truly wants, she continually settles for lesser goals in order to avoid pain. In turn, she forfeits the personality she wants and develops one that is nothing more than a coping style.

You may not have a single thorn that changes your life to such an extreme extent, but all of our lives reflect thorns and bits of glass. Our thorns are emotional. They are the painful experiences—both in our past and future—that we're avoiding.

Our true and authentic self isn't who we currently are. It isn't our limitations. Instead, it is our deepest-held aspirations, dreams, and goals.

Rather than facing our fears, and rather than facing the truth, we avoid them.

Rather than creating the life we want, we build the life that allows our problems to exist unresolved.

Rather than becoming the person we want to become, we stay the person we are.

Rather than adapting our personality to match our goals, we adapt our goals to match our current and limited personality.

How have negative experiences shaped you?

Where do you have a fixed mindset?

Where have you built your life around your thorns?

What goals are you pursuing to avoid dealing with your trauma?

How would your life be different if the trauma was gone?

What life would you ideally choose for yourself?

Who is your ideal future self, regardless of what you've been in the past or what has happened to you?

Moving Past Trauma

> I always wanted to be better, wanted more. I can't really
> explain it, other than that I loved the game but had a very
> short memory. That fueled me until the day I hung up
> my sneakers.
>
> —*Kobe Bryant*

In psychology, a *refractory period* is the amount of time it takes to emotionally recover and move on from an experience. Small frustrations, such as getting cut off on the road or getting in an argument with your spouse, may take a few minutes or hours to recover from. Some events, though, may take months, years, or even decades to let go of. Indeed, some events are never outgrown.

Becoming psychologically flexible enables you to *shorten the length* of refractory periods—even when really painful or difficult experiences happen. You become psychologically flexible by being in touch with your emotions but not completely absorbed by them. You hold your thoughts and emotions loosely as you actively pursue meaningful goals.

In professional basketball, players don't have time to get upset and discouraged if they miss a shot. They may be disappointed or embarrassed when they miss, but ultimately, they need to get back in the game and stay both attentive to the moment and committed to the goal of helping their team win, regardless of how they are feeling.

If they linger on the emotion of the missed shot, they won't be able to operate fully on the court, which creates more problems for themselves and their team. If they emotionally attach to what happened, they may avoid taking the shot next time out of fear or negative expectation. They're then stuck in the past rather than acting as their future self.

The less you hold on to mistakes or painful experiences, the better you're able to adapt to what the situation requires and perform in order to achieve your goals. What happened in the past doesn't impact the next thing you do, or stop you from being entirely present in *this moment*.

The more psychologically flexible you are, the faster you can let things go. The less psychologically flexible you are, the longer you hold on to even small things.

Rosalie still remembers her art class the same way she did nearly fifty years ago. Her memory of the experience hasn't changed or been recontextualized. Because the context of that memory hasn't changed, the meaning of the experience hasn't changed. As a result, Rosalie still sees the teacher who hurt her feelings as rude, and she still sees herself as lacking the potential to create art. None of these elements of the experience or her memory have changed.

If, however, she had flexibly moved forward from that event rather than attaching to it, she might have learned to illustrate her own stories. She might have produced dozens of books that have been read by many children. Over time, her memory of that experience would have changed in meaning. She might even have forgotten about the experience altogether. It might not have held enough meaning to be worth remembering, let alone become identity-defining.

When a person remains stuck in an emotional refractory period following a difficult experience, they continue seeing and experiencing life from their *initial reaction* to the experience. Therefore, day after day, they continue reconstructing the emotions of the experience. They don't regulate and reframe how they see and feel about the event.

Trauma becomes a rut.

As the author Dr. Joe Dispenza states:

> If you keep that refractory period going for weeks and months, you've developed a temperament. If you keep that same refractory period going on for years, it's called a personality trait. When we begin to develop personality traits based on our emotions, we're living in the past, and that's where we get stuck. Teaching ourselves and our children to shorten the refractory period frees us to move through life without obstruction.

Empathetic Witness: How to Transform Trauma

> You're only as sick as your secrets.
>
> —*Alcoholics Anonymous*

Trauma is an interpretation of an experience tied to a severely painful emotion. However, experiences that become traumatic don't necessarily need to continue that way. Although an initial reaction may be highly negative or debilitating, all painful experiences can be reframed, reinterpreted, and ultimately used as growing experiences.

In order for painful experiences to be growing experiences rather than debilitating ones, you can't bottle up and internalize the pain. You can't have a "fragile identity," wherein you avoid mistakes or getting feedback. You need to face your emotions personally and be willing to share them with others. By facing your emotions and experiences, you change them.

That day over fifty years ago when Rosalie experienced her trauma, she went home and told no one about it. She bottled up her emotions and kept them private. She made a rash judgment about the experience and never got help reframing it. She quit on her goal. And that's why it was traumatic.

Dr. Peter Levine, a renowned trauma researcher, said, "Trauma is not what happens to us, but what we hold inside in the absence of an empathetic witness."

Rosalie didn't have an empathetic witness. She didn't have someone listen to her trauma and help her to reframe it.

Emotions are difficult to express for anyone, especially painful emotions. And like so many others, Rosalie kept her pain to herself and committed to a lesser future. She didn't have someone to help confirm the idea that *she could do it,* that her desired future self could be real. She didn't have a coach or mentor to help her push through the pain of a single "failure" or roadblock and continue advancing toward her dreams. She didn't even have a friend to help her rethink that art class experience.

"Maybe that teacher didn't mean to make you feel bad?" a friend might have told Rosalie over lunch. But that conversation never happened.

As is the case with many painful experiences, they are bottled and made secretive. Consider the statistics of a much worse form of trauma: sexual abuse. Research shows that *up to 90 percent* of sexual abuse survivors don't report the abuse.

The more painful the emotional experience, the more likely we are to bottle it up and internalize it. And with this emotional bottling comes a premature cognitive commitment and fixed mindset about who we are. Rather than emotions expressed and reframed, the past becomes something too painful to think about. The avoidance of that pain can create a lifetime of addiction in attempts to numb oneself to both the pain of the past and the pain of pursuing a desired future self.

An empathetic witness could have helped Rosalie alter her experience and even helped her express how she felt *to the art teacher*. Doing so would have been an incredible act of courage. It might have completely changed Rosalie's life. She might have discovered that the teacher had no intention of causing her pain. She might have seen him differently and totally reframed the meaning of that event. She could have come to see him as a caring instructor who only wanted her to succeed. And even if it turned out that he did have limited views of her, she might have come to realize the truth of Eleanor Roosevelt's words: "No one can make you feel inferior without your consent."

But she never had any of these conversations or transformational experiences. And as a result, she is still defined by her initial response. She's spent the past fifty years convincing herself of the truth of her experience and confirming the bias that came with it.

One exciting thing, though, is that during our few days together, Rosalie's mind showed signs of expanding. Simply talking about that event, reframing it in her mind, and focusing on her desire to write and draw for children seemed to have an impact.

And for the first time in fifty years, Rosalie drew a picture. It was only a first step, and the process of healing a lifelong trauma will continue to take time and effort, but Rosalie was able to take that initial step simply by having an empathetic witness.

Contrast Rosalie's struggle with her trauma with my wife's journey of overcoming hers. During her first year of college, my wife married a man whose goals and ambitions matched hers exactly, but unbeknownst to her, he harbored extreme anger and struggles with addiction.

Just weeks after they were married, he hit her for the first time. She lived in her hometown just miles from her parents but didn't speak up. She was in shock from the experience and also afraid of her parents' potential judgment. Maybe they'd be disappointed in her for her husband's behavior. Or maybe, maybe, they'd be disappointed in her for not dealing with it herself. Those were her thoughts in the emotional shock of her trauma.

She kept everything secret. She tried to be "strong."

Three years later, living across the country, what had begun as occasional abuse had escalated to daily rampages that left permanent scars.

Much later, when Lauren had left that relationship and she and I were dating, we decided to do some couples counseling in preparation for marriage. During therapy, the counselor told me that Lauren's prior marriage would be something I'd deal with the rest of my life. I should expect to trigger her at any time, and I'd need to be empathetic and patient.

Lauren didn't believe what the counselor was saying. She had already decided to not let the labels of "divorced," "abused," or "victim" follow her. Her former self and trauma weren't going to define her future self. Anyone who meets her today would never believe she spent years living in quiet fear surrounded by emotional and physical abuse.

She has faced these issues and dealt with them, head-on and completely. She spoke openly with counselors, friends, and family, and with herself through her journal. She intentionally spoke about her trauma when in safe and uplifting environments. In this way, her memory of her trauma was changed and influenced.

She pulled the thorn out.

Her trauma transformed into incredible growth.

She's no longer controlled by the abuse.

Her future self calls the shots.

Her past, and all the pain involved, happened for her, not to her. Her view of that period of her life is one of gratitude and peace, not resentment. She's forgiven her former self and her ex-husband.

When others approach her and ask how they can help family and friends in situations similar to hers, she always answers with the same response: Listen to them, ask good questions, never judge, and never advise. These are the key principles to being an empathetic witness.

An empathetic witness is what we all need to flatten whatever trauma we face. As the renowned therapist Lynn Wilson said, "It is this honest connection between two human beings that, in the end, makes what we endured together understandable and meaningful."

Lynn would know. In 1991, she coauthored a book called *The Flock: The Autobiography of a Multiple Personality* with her twenty-six-year-old client, Joan Frances Casey, who had been so traumatized that she developed twenty-four different personalities in an extreme case of multiple personality disorder. Through deep and committed work and the healing connection between the two of them, and with Lynn as the empathetic witness, Joan's profoundly fragmented self healed into a cohesive and singular one.

Until the day Lauren left her abusive situation, she had never considered that she would actually do so. The abuse had become so routine that her mind had turned off the reality of the situation. She didn't feel a fight-or-flight instinct; she was simply frozen. But on that day, she went to her sister-in-law's house for a short vacation. That is where she met her empathetic witness, Natalie.

Although Natalie had never met Lauren before, she was quickly able to see her trauma and began listening. She asked Lauren questions Lauren had never thought to ask herself before. Natalie was interested in Lauren and never judged her. Lauren quickly learned to trust Natalie, and after they spent a few days together, Natalie stayed up one night and wrote a narrative in Lauren's words. It had none of Natalie's thoughts, opinions, or judgment. Only Lauren's own words, held up to her like a mirror.

When Lauren read this narrative, she was in complete shock. It was clear to her that she could *never go back*. Not back to her husband, and not back to being that person.

She was done.

She called her dad on the spot and read Natalie's narrative to him. He booked a flight immediately and together they packed up her belongings.

It is never too late to find, or to be, an empathetic witness to trauma. In fact, if you're serious about transforming your life, you need to surround yourself with a whole new cast of friends, mentors, and supporters. You need people you can talk with openly about your struggles.

You need people who can help you get to your own next level. Otherwise, you're going to hit some emotional experiences, bottle them up, and plateau or decline as a person.

Molehills can become mountains if you don't have an empathetic witness to help you process and reframe your experiences. A true empathetic witness encourages you to decide what you can do to move forward.

Courage is always required to face the truth and move forward in your life.

Courage transforms trauma.

Encouragement facilitates courage.

Getting encouragement from others in your life helps you act courageously yourself. This is why you need encouraging people in your life.

> **Quick exercise:** List two or three people in your life who have been your biggest encouragers.
>
> How have they encouraged you?
>
> Why has it been so impactful?
>
> Reach out to them and openly thank them for their help in your life.

Often, it is incredibly small and simple acts that can have the biggest impact on our lives. For instance, Rich Beverage was a key empathetic witness in my life, someone who encouraged me when I was down. At nineteen years old, I had given up on my goal of serving a church mission. Rich, a former church leader, reached out to me and took me out to lunch a few times. It was a small gesture, but incredibly impactful. He helped me realize that my mistakes and circumstances shouldn't stop me from taking action on my future. His encouragement helped me courageously make the decision I'd almost lost hope in.

In a 2019 interview, TV personality Lisa Ling explained the importance of having a team of people around her to do the work she does. She hosts the CNN show *This Is Life*, which is radically raw and open. Ling often interviews people with profound emotional pain and struggles. For example, she once interviewed a seventeen-year-old girl who was sold into commercial sex exploitation at age eleven. During the interview, this girl said that at that age she would regularly call police officers, begging them to arrest her so she could have a safe place to sleep.

This is just one example of countless, painfully real conversations Ling has. The aftermath, as was the case with the seventeen-year-old girl, is that Ling and her small team are left sobbing and crying together, due to the overwhelming reality of the interviews and stories. As Ling recalled:

> She ended up having to console me because I had just been so overwhelmed with grief, and after that interview, my team and I, we just kind of like huddled together and just, we all cried together. Again, this is five men and me and we just had to let it out. It was just so devastating. . . . Having these teams who are with you along the way has really been my salvation, because if I were alone doing this, I don't know that I would have been able to survive all these years because it is so emotionally taxing, but having these people by my side—and, really, my team consists of the most sensitive, incredible people, men and women—has been what has gotten me through all of it.

Ling is doing powerful, important, and emotional work. She is smart because she knows she couldn't handle what she's doing on her own. She has a group of empathetic witnesses to help her through.

If you're serious about seeking growth in your life, you'll need a team of empathetic witnesses around you as well. You don't need to be doing the level of emotional work that Ling is doing. All growth toward big goals and important work is emotionally taxing. Don't go it alone. Have a team you can huddle around when you're fried, torn, burned out, scared, or broken.

If you're going to create a powerful future, you'll experience an intense amount of failures, heartaches, bad days, and pain along the way. You need a team of empathetic witnesses. You need people who encourage you to keep going—people who encourage you to dream big and encourage your work when others don't understand.

David Osborn is a highly successful entrepreneur and real estate investor. He's worth over $100 million. He attributes much of his success to a small group of "accountability partners." These four friends have regularly gotten together for over a decade to support and hold each other accountable.

One of the things they do as a part of their regular get-togethers, which often take place in exotic environments around the world, is read their "One Sheet" to each other. On this One Sheet they have all of the important and intimate metrics of their lives on open display. Financially, they share their net worth, income, how much they have recently given to charity, amount of passive income, and so on. There are also exact numbers on body fat percentage, muscle mass, and other health and fitness levels, including blood work. They even provide metrics for their personal life, such as their rated level of happiness personally and how they rate their relationships with their spouses.

In addition to openly sharing exactly where they are numerically in all the key areas of their lives, their One Sheet reveals how much those numbers have changed over the previous year and where they want them to be a year into the future.

It takes courage to be honest and "naked" with others. Osborn and his "tribe" see accountability as the most powerful force in the world. They are empathetic witnesses, coaches, and accountability partners for each other, and they attribute much of their success—which all four have experienced rare and high levels of—to their accountability group.

> Who are three important empathetic witnesses in your life right now?
>
> What other people could you add, or do you need, as empathetic witnesses?
>
> Who could you get on your team, right now, to help you get where you want to go?
>
> How much accountability and vulnerability do you currently have?

Your "team" should include many different members. I remember when I started working with my financial advisor. It initially felt weird being so honest about my finances. I felt insecure about where I currently was. But my advisor helped me think differently about money. He helped me clarify my goals and set up amazing systems to achieve my goals. He's just one member of my team. But he's been an empathetic witness.

The bigger my future self becomes, the more empathetic witnesses I need in my circle to help me get there. As leadership expert and author Robin Sharma has said, "The bigger the dream, the more important the team."

Becoming an Empathetic Witness to Those Around You

In addition to seeking empathetic witnesses in your own life, you can and should seek to be the empathetic witness that others around you so desperately need. You can expect that pretty much everyone you know has bottled-up emotional pain. In the words of university president and religious leader Dr. Henry Eyring, "When you meet someone, treat them as if they were in serious trouble and you will be right more than half the time."

Any experience or perspective can be transformed through compassionate conversations. Research shows that when empathetic listening is done well, mutual trust and understanding occur. It must be done in a safe and collaborative environment where both parties are heard, and where both parties ultimately create a new shared past and future.

When being listened to in an empathetic and loving way, the speaker hears themself talk and gains clarity about their problem. They become better equipped to find a resolution. An emotional burden is lifted, and they feels less stressed and confused. Their self-esteem and self-awareness increase.

Being an empathetic witness is about being interested, not interesting. Empathetic listening can't be done in haste. It must be done out of love. Even if you will never truly understand where the other person is coming from, you need to *want to understand*. When done correctly, the listener's core motivation is to understand and encourage.

Time is allowed for each person to open up and process their perspectives. Solutions or advice are *not* presented, at least initially. Instead, open-ended and sincere questions are asked. When the questions have been answered, the listener continues asking for more information and insight, with questions like:

"Can you explain more for me?"

"What do you mean by that?"

"Why was that part so important?"

"Have you given up on the idea of a better future?"

"What positives have come from this?"

"How will your future be different because of this?"

"What can you do now to move forward?"

"How can I help?"

After the other person has spoken, you rephrase or repeat back what they said to ensure you've heard correctly. Then ask for more. Your questions are real and genuine, based on deep and connected listening.

Trust is everything in relationships. Don't attempt to build trust in haste. Once it is built, anything becomes possible. Once it is destroyed, even the simplest of things can become insurmountable.

Transforming trauma is ultimately about *rebuilding trust*. When trust is lost, so are confidence and hope. Rosalie needed to trust herself enough to pursue a difficult goal.

When confidence and hope are lost, the future is gone and the past becomes of utmost importance. Trauma shatters imagination. Trust and confidence are the foundation of imagination and the possibility for change.

Trauma can happen in any relationship. People will make mistakes. Apologies must come and forgiveness must be granted to move forward. But it must happen together. Neither party's perspective of the past is objective, but rather subjective in meaning. The memory of the past must be created together, through empathetic and loving understanding.

Any trauma can be transformed. The past can be changed. Even in relationships that seem stuck and are disintegrating.

Are any of your relationships stuck in the past?

Have former experiences created a fixed mindset in any of your relationships?

Who are three people you could be an empathetic witness to, right now?

Conclusion

Trauma is at the core of who we are as people. If we transform it, we can become unstoppable in what we're trying to accomplish. If we don't transform our trauma, then our very lives become its by-product.

A cornerstone of trauma is that it is isolated, internalized, and then avoided. The initial emotional reaction—which is negative, painful, and likely paralyzing—becomes the filter through which the memory is stored.

Healthy memories change over time. A growing person continually has a changing past, expanding in meaning and usefulness.

In order to move on from painful experiences, you can't avoid them. You need to face them. Writing down and organizing your thoughts and emotions in your journal is essential and powerful. You can get your thoughts and feelings out of mind and onto paper. By facing your emotions and negative experiences, you change them.

Still, you need an outsider's perspective to help you reframe your experience. As the saying goes, "You can't read the label from inside the jar." An empathetic witness, someone who isn't trying to give you advice, but is altruistically sitting with you and listening, can give you the space to openly express your feelings. In this way, your feelings are free to be transformed. A professional counselor is a good option for an empathetic witness.

If you have any negative or painful experiences you've yet to transform, it's time to find an empathetic witness—hopefully many. It's time to transform your trauma and past. It's time to move beyond your initial reaction and become psychologically flexible. Reach out to someone you trust. Be as honest as possible in sharing your story and experiences.

Also, openly and honestly describe your future self, your true desires. Be open to share about the potentially "lesser goals" you've been pursuing or living as a by-product of your trauma.

Finally, if there are important people in your life who need forgiving, or need a deeper connection from you or by you, then go and have those conversations. You'll be shocked by how quickly the feelings of the past will dissipate and change. It will feel like you've just come up for breath, and you didn't realize how suffocated your life had become.

CHAPTER 4

Shift Your Story

> The stories of our lives, far from being fixed narratives, are under constant revision. The slender threads of causality are rewoven and reinterpreted as we attempt to explain to ourselves and others how we became the people we are. . . . This is why in the initial stages of psychotherapy it is important to listen to the patient's story uncritically. Contained in those memories are not just the events, but also the meaning they have for that particular person.
>
> —*Gordon Livingston, MD*

Buzz Aldrin was the Apollo Lunar Module pilot on the Apollo 11 mission. He stepped down onto the dusty surface of the moon just a few seconds after Neil Armstrong became the first man to set foot on the moon and utter those historic words, "One small step for man." But what should have been an incredible, positive experience for Aldrin nearly ruined his life.

During the three-week quarantine then required of astronauts upon returning from space, Aldrin immediately began an alcohol bender that didn't end for over nine years. His marriage of twenty-one years quickly decayed and ended, and his prestigious military career concluded on bad terms. At his lowest point, he was working at a Cadillac dealership in Beverly Hills and didn't make a single sale in six months.

One night, Aldrin was drunk and his girlfriend locked him out of her house. In his rage, he pounded her door down and broke into her home. Terrified and in shock, she called the police. Aldrin was arrested.

How did this all happen? How could someone as successful and brilliant as Buzz Aldrin experience such a negative shift?

Aldrin himself gave the answer in his 2009 autobiography, *Magnificent Desolation*: "The transition from 'astronaut preparing to accomplish the next big thing' to 'astronaut telling about the last big thing' did not come easily to me. . . . What does a man do for an encore?"

During the return flight from the moon, Aldrin became absorbed in negative thinking and emotions. Staring down at Earth, he lost his imagination. Nothing could top what he had just done. His future was over.

I will never outlive this, he thought.

He had peaked at thirty-nine years old. Such thinking terrified him, so he tried to drink away his pain.

Compare Buzz Aldrin's story with that of basketball player Giannis Antetokounmpo.

Antetokounmpo grew up poor in Greece. He and his brother actually had to share the single pair of basketball shoes their family could afford. His brother would wear the shoes during the early game and Antetokounmpo would wear the same shoes during the late game.

Antetokounmpo recently signed a major deal with Nike, and now his signature shoes are being worn by tens of thousands of kids throughout the world. During the 2018–2019 season, he was awarded the NBA's Most Valuable Player award. In an interview, ESPN commentator Rachel Nichols asked Antetokounmpo if it had sunk in that he was the MVP.

"I'm really happy about it, I'm not going to lie," he said. "But I don't ever want to hear about it again for the rest of my life. It's a great accomplishment and great honor. But, you know, that's in the past now."

"Wait, you mean you don't ever want to hear the words 'MVP' again?" Nichols asked, surprised.

"No, I think it's gotten too much. Usually, when you share that, you tend to relax. If I keep thinking, 'I'm the MVP of this league,' then what's going to happen? I'm just going to relax. And I do not want to do that. I'm proud of it. But let's go for the next goal."

Antetokounmpo is defined by his goals, not his previous accomplishments or failures. He's defined by *what he's going to do next*. He's chasing his future self, and that's why he's continually successful.

According to Dan Sullivan, the founder of Strategic Coach, when your "status" becomes more important than your "growth," you usually stop growing. However, when growth *is your genuine motive*, then you usually end up getting lots of status. But you won't be attached to it. And you'll definitely be willing to destroy a former status to create a new one. As Sullivan says, "Always make your future bigger than your past."

If you're honest with yourself, you may find that you are primarily motivated by a particular *status*. Once you obtain that status—such as a particular job title, income level, or relationship—your motivation shifts from *approach-oriented* to *avoid-oriented*. Rather than approaching a new and expansive future self, your primary concern becomes to maintain or protect your current status or identity by avoiding failure. You'll stop being courageous. You'll plateau, and the energy and zest that was your growing personality fizzles out into something far less inspiring.

Without a future self that has outgrown and outdone your current self, life starts to lose its meaning.

Condoleezza Rice served as the sixty-sixth US secretary of state. She was also the first female African American secretary of state and the second female secretary of state. She has continually defied the odds throughout her life and career. One of the reasons she's been so successful and innovative is due to a philosophy she holds. In her own words, "I firmly believe you should never spend any of your time being the 'former' anything."

The idea that you should "never be the 'former' anything" conveys in one phrase the entire premise of this book. Whether you *were* an astronaut or a drug addict, you should never *be* the former anything. Both trauma and achievement can have a powerful impact on your personality. But whichever you experience, you should never get stuck in the past, nor let your past define you.

Your authentic self is your future self. Who you aspire to be.

For so long, Buzz Aldrin's "mission" was to stand on the moon. It was the purpose or goal he built his identity, choices, and environment around. But then he got stuck in his status after "fulfilling his purpose." From his perspective, there was no way he was going to outdo his former self, so he threw in the towel on his future. Without a meaningful purpose, his life went into a tailspin.

Aldrin, someone whose goals and imagination pushed him to the moon, went totally blank on his future self.

Giannis Antetokounmpo took the opposite path. *Within weeks* of being named MVP, he emotionally detached from the status and put his focus on the next goal.

This doesn't mean he isn't happy or grateful. What it means is that he hasn't become emotionally attached to an outcome or an identity. His vision of himself remains in the future, not the past. And as a result, while others around him will plateau, he will not. He continues living, rather than existing.

For the rest of this chapter, you'll learn why we formulate narratives and stories to shape the meaning of our experiences. You'll learn to reframe your narrative to be future-focused—on who you intend to be—as Giannis and others, like Elon Musk, do. This is a rare skill, and part of why they are so successful.

With these new skills in place, you'll be challenged to *reframe your narrative* so that your past isn't keeping you stuck but pushing you forward. Your past is happening for you, not to you. After reading this chapter, you'll be challenged to have your future self be the story you tell others in explaining yourself, not your former self.

Who are you?

Creating "Meaning" Through Stories

Recently, my wife and oldest son, Kaleb, who is eleven, were out walking our two seven-month-old twin girls. Kaleb was manning the stroller. They were on a country road with lots of shrubbery and ditches on either side of the road.

I needed to chat with Lauren before leaving for work, so I drove around to find them. I pulled up beside Lauren, and we began talking. Kaleb stood by listening.

The rocky road we were on was slightly slanted downward on the edges. Within about twenty seconds of starting the conversation, I noticed the stroller beginning to drift toward a ditch. I yelled for Kaleb to grab it!

He did his best, but the momentum was too much. He was getting pulled down into the ditch with the girls.

Immediately, Zorah was crying, as she had fallen out of her stroller seat. She wasn't strapped in. Phoebe was strapped in and stayed in her seat.

Luckily, the fall wasn't bad. Zorah was fine, just scared. But Kaleb was noticeably shaken by the experience. He was crying, staring at the ground, and not making eye contact even after a few prods. I could see that in the midst of his emotions, he was defining the meaning of this experience. And given that his emotions were negative, the meaning he was forming was also negative.

I didn't want this for Kaleb. I wanted to help him regulate his emotions and become psychologically flexible. I wanted him to proactively and healthily frame this experience, not for it to absorb him.

Meaning is shaped during emotional experiences. According to the famed psychologist Dr. Roy Baumeister, meaning is a mental representation of relationships between events or things. "Meaning connects things," Baumeister explains.

Dr. Crystal Park, an expert on the psychology of meaning and meaning-making, argues that human beings create meaning from our experiences by connecting three things:

- First, we **define the cause** of the event or experience. ("What just happened?")
- Second, we **link that cause with our own identity.** ("What does this experience say about me?")
- Finally, we **link that cause and our identity with the bigger picture** of how the world and universe work. ("What does this experience and who I am say about the world?")

Creating meaning is fundamental to who we are and who we become. Our personality, in large part, is based on the meaning we've placed on former experiences. It's based on the meaning we give to various goals or values. It's based on what we focus on. Our personality is even based on the meaning we place on small things, like humor or music or style or interests.

Creating meaning is something we do instinctively. But it has a dark side. If we are not intentional about the meanings we form, we can generate a premature cognitive commitment about ourselves.

I'm a bad person.

I'm an introvert.

I'm never going to live my dreams.

I'm not good with people.

I don't like people like her.

Meaning-making can, if you're not intentional, lead to a fixed mindset. Trauma, for instance, isn't the event itself but a meaning you take or create from it. Something terrible happened, but what made it traumatic *was in your interpretation.*

Take, for example, Sean Stephenson, a giant of a man born with osteogenesis imperfecta, a bone disorder that left him three feet tall and in a wheelchair from birth. Stephenson's perspective was, and his last words before dying were, "This happened for me, not to me." He had fallen out of his wheelchair, hit his head, and was in a great deal of pain. Moments before drifting to the other side, those were his words. That was his interpretation, not only of the incident that killed him but of his entire life, as potentially traumatic as it was or could have been.

Trauma is the meaning you give to an event or experience, and how that meaning shapes your view of yourself, your future, and the world at large. The meaning you formed during former "traumas" is now driving your personality, your choices, and your goals.

Until you change that meaning.

Think about it for a second: Why do you define yourself the way you do? Why are you the way you are? Why do you like or dislike certain things? Why are your pursuing what you're pursuing?

It all comes down to the meaning you've shaped of your former experiences, as well as the identity you've formed as a result.

The meaning we derive from our experiences and the information we gather shapes our worldview. It's important to note that as people, we usually shape meaning first about ourselves, and then use our self-image as the lens through which we view the world. As Dr. Stephen Covey said, "We see the world, not as it is, but as we are."

If you have a negative view of yourself, then you probably have a negative view of the world. If you have a positive view of yourself, then you probably have a positive view of the world. *The world is viewed through the lens of your identity.*

You only see, or selectively attend to, what is meaningful and relevant to you. This is why Andre Norman stopped seeing all the criminal behavior around him in prison after Harvard became his purpose and identity. It's also why Aldrin stopped seeing opportunities for growth once he got trapped in the status of his former self.

Your view of the world says more about you than it does about the world. Your view of the past says more about you than it does about the past. Consequently, you should formulate meaning *based on your desired future self.* This requires being *intentional about your interpretation* of your experiences, even your hard ones.

How would my future self respond to this experience?

What would they think about it?

What would they do about it?

How could they turn this to their benefit?

This is happening for me, not to me.

Kaleb, in the heat of his emotions, was formulating meaning to understand his experience of letting go of the stroller. Although nothing bad happened to the girls, it had the potential to be traumatic for Kaleb and leave lasting harm. As part of the meaning-making process, Kaleb's thoughts and feelings likely went through the three stages of meaning-making: (1) defining a cause, (2) shaping his own identity, and (3) shaping his view of the world through his identity.

Examples of cause-effect thoughts could include:

Was it my fault the stroller began rolling because I wasn't holding on to it?

Why wasn't I holding on to it?

Was this Dad's fault because he stopped Mom's and my walk?

Why was Dad distracting us from our walk?

Was this because we were walking on a country road?

Why did Mom want us to walk so much? I just wanted to stay back at camp.

Examples of identity-forming thoughts based on his cause-effect thinking include:

I don't like being with my parents.

I'm not a good brother.

I don't like going on walks with Mom.

I'm not going to do stuff like this anymore.

My baby sisters are too fragile and not fun.

After thinking about the event and himself, Kaleb creates "global meaning" about the bigger picture of life. Examples may include:

Going on walks is dangerous.

The world is dangerous.

Life is horrible.

Dad always ruins things.

This meaning-making process all takes only a moment in the

brain. More than thoughts, these cause-and-effect scenarios reflect Kaleb's initial emotional reaction to the event. Without the skill of emotional regulation, which takes time and practice, and without the help of an empathetic witness to help him proactively and healthily frame his experiences, despite his initial reaction, he may reactively and negatively create meaning from this experience.

Human beings are fundamentally meaning-making machines. We create meaning in order to comprehend our lives. When you understand this fact, you start to see it everywhere. We create meaning even in the smallest and most mundane of experiences, which have an impact on our identity and worldview. Every small experience counts.

For example, I was on a long drive recently, and out of nowhere, I had to go to the bathroom *really bad*. It took about five minutes to find an exit. During those five minutes, I had several thoughts racing through my head.

This is ridiculous.

This sucks.

Why is this happening to me?

Then I began to notice my thinking and became intentional about it, which is a key technique of what psychologists call *emotional regulation*. As you become more intentional about your life, you start to see small moments like this as "practice," or "reps," for being who you want to be. If you can't handle the small moments when the stakes are low, you won't show up effectively in the big ones.

Life is practice.

When regulating challenging emotions, you can define the meaning of your experiences intentionally. This is the exact opposite of how people often handle their emotions and the meaning-making process. Most thoughts are governed *by emotions,* particularly in emotionally heated situations. Those thoughts are reactive and un-intentional, but go on to become the long-term meaning and narrative held by the person.

Instead, your thoughts, or, more specifically, your goals, should govern your emotions, even when the initial emotions triggered by the experience are difficult.

The better you get at emotional regulation in both small and big experiences, the more psychologically flexible you become. As you become more psychologically flexible, your emotions and experiences stop defining you in a reactive way. You're enabled to move forward in a goal-directed and value-centered way, holding your initial emotions and thoughts loosely and becoming better at directing your emotions and thoughts.

The first step of emotional regulation is **identifying and labeling your emotions** as you're experiencing them (the more descriptive the better). You can't manage something you're not aware of.

The second step of emotional regulation is understanding the difference between **primary emotions** and **secondary emotions**.

Primary emotions are your initial reactions to external events. You shouldn't judge them. They are natural reactions to things around us. For example, being sad when a loved one dies, or being frustrated in traffic, are natural initial responses.

A secondary emotion is when you feel something *about the feeling itself*. For example, you may feel anger about being hurt, or shame about your anxiety. Secondary emotions increase the intensity of your reactions and can push you into destructive behaviors. Hence, part of becoming psychologically flexible is holding your initial reaction loosely—not taking it too seriously or overly identifying with it, but acknowledging it, labeling it, and then deciding how you want to interpret and feel about the experience.

The third step of emotional regulation is **letting go of negative emotions**. Accepting and acknowledging that you're feeling negative is key to letting the feeling go, rather than pretending you're not feeling it. You then want to step back from the emotion and consider the consequences of acting on it. Usually, the consequences aren't in line with the values and goals of your future self.

People often make stupid decisions because they act based on their emotions in the moment, rather than on the consequences that will come after. For example, binge-eating cookies while stressed may initially feel good but will ultimately create negative consequences. It is the consequences you want to think about, because they will determine your feelings in the long term. The consequences are what create your future self.

Given that Kaleb is only eleven years old, he isn't yet adept at emotional regulation. Lauren and I are trying to help him foster his ability to not bottle things up, but rather to safely and openly express himself. Expressing emotions openly and honestly is key to emotional regulation and becoming psychologically flexible. The better you get at expressing emotions, the better you'll handle them and positively respond to them.

Kaleb needed an empathetic witness. The last thing he needed in this moment of emotion was a lecture. We told him that he did his best to help the girls, and that everything was okay. We let him hold and comfort Zorah, and praised him for being a comfort to her. "Accidents happen," we said.

We helped him express his emotions, and we decided as a family what to do about the experience. We turned the meaning of the experience into something positive and constructive rather than negative.

Fundamental to the meaning-making process is developing stories. We understand the meaning of our experiences *through* stories. We understand our identity through stories. We have stories for our lives, for specific events, even for a given day. The more intentional you get about your life, the more you become the author of the story. You shape the meaning of your past. You also shape the meaning of current and future experiences in order to have the story you want for your past.

Rather than telling the story of Kaleb's blunder, we chose to tell the story of his heroic rescue. As the wizard teaches in the musical *Wicked,* "Is one a crusader or ruthless invader? It's all in which label is able to persist." We moved past the primary emotions of fear and failure and took the narrative into our own hands.

> How much of your current narrative is based on primary emotions, your initial reaction to various events or experiences?
>
> What is the meaning you continue to give to previous events that no longer serve the story you wish to tell about yourself?
>
> What is the story of "you"?
>
> Who are you?
>
> Why are you the person you are?

These are questions we will explore throughout the chapter. As you will find, you can and should be the one shaping this story.

Your Past Is Fiction:
It's *Your* Story—Get Creative!

Ken Arlen grew up in the 1970s, and during his junior year of high school he started smoking a lot of marijuana. To cover up the smell, he smoked cigarettes because, although they weren't thrilled about it, his parents didn't really mind. Cigarettes weren't as negatively viewed back then.

Ken's smoking continued throughout his senior year of high school and his four years of college. During college, he got to the point where he was smoking a pack of cigarettes a day. In recounting his story to me, Ken said he actually believed it was physically impossible to drink a beer without smoking a cigarette at the same time. He couldn't even drink a cup of coffee without smoking.

He and his friends all tried quitting on multiple occasions during college, but to no avail. "It was an ongoing theme," he said. "I mean, I probably tried quitting at least twenty times and was unsuccessful."

Smoking was a fundamental aspect of his identity and tied to everything he did. He smoked when he studied, when he woke up in the morning, when he was with his friends. He really wanted to quit, because he knew it wasn't healthy. He knew it was a bad habit and that he was addicted to the nicotine. He also had the goal of playing trumpet.

When he got out of college, he was in a state of transition. He moved to Madison, Wisconsin, and got a job as an orderly in a paraplegic ward.

At the hospital, there was a lounge where orderlies hung out, and smoking was acceptable there. On Ken's first day on the job, he walked into the lounge and one of the other orderlies pulled out a cigarette and offered him one.

He said, "No, thanks. Don't smoke. Never have, never will."

That event occurred over forty years ago. Ken has never smoked a cigarette since.

Ken changed his narrative. He changed his past, and that allowed him to have a new identity in his new environment.

Firstly, he was in a new environment where no one knew of his former identity as a smoker. He also explained that the decision to say he wasn't a smoker was impulsive yet strategic. By publicly declaring himself as a nonsmoker to his coworkers, he put himself in a position where smoking around them would be incongruent.

"I think there was some wisdom in my subconscious that helped me come up with the idea, because I knew a lot of habits and addiction are a response to peer pressure and environment. I wanted to be a nonsmoker in that environment."

It took about a week for the nicotine cravings to go away, which weren't that difficult to deal with given that most of Ken's time was spent at work where he assumed the identity of a nonsmoker. After that initial week, *he never thought about smoking again.*

He's the storyteller.

The Gap and the Gain: Reframing Your Narrative

According to the theory of "narrative identity" developed by scholar and researcher Dr. Dan McAdams, we all form our identity by integrating our life experiences into an internalized evolving story. The story gives a sense of unity and purpose to our lives.

This life narrative integrates our reconstructed past, perceived present, and imagined future. All three coexist at the same time. Hence, from an experiential standpoint, the past, present, and future are not separate and linear but holistic and co-occurring. Your past, present, and future are all happening *right now*—at least in your mind.

The stories we hold of ourselves are continually evolving and changing based on the experiences we are having. The "facts" about your past don't necessarily change, but the story you tell yourself about those facts absolutely can and does. And when you revise your own history, you may leave out and ultimately forget certain "facts" that once played a dominant role in your story. Perhaps certain facts weren't actually facts but merely your former perspective.

Instead of creating a narrative that serves them, people often get trapped in stories based on their initial reaction to an experience.

A fundamental aspect of "reframing" your narrative of the past is shifting what was formerly defined as a negative experience into a positive one. You may be scratching your head and asking yourself, "Why would I want to do this? If the experience was negative, why would I pretend that it was positive?"

"Positive" and "negative" aren't facts, but *meanings*.

The meaning you place on past events determines who you are and what your future is. Changing how you view your past is essential to upgrading your identity and future. Fundamental to changing your identity is also changing your story. A new future creates a new past.

Having studied this for over a decade, I've never seen a more useful reframing technique than what Dan Sullivan calls "the gap and the gain." According to Sullivan, living in "the gap" occurs when you focus on what's missing.

When you're in the gap, you can't enjoy or comprehend the benefits in your life. All you're focused on is why something wasn't how you thought it should have been. For instance, you might live in a great house. But if you're in the gap, then all you might see is what's wrong with your house. You may have an amazing partner but only see what you believe to be wrong or missing in them.

That's the gap.

You might have great kids, but only see where they come up short.

You might have made huge progress over the past ninety days on your goals, but only see where things didn't go according to plan.

Compare living in the gap to living in "the gain." Instead of constantly measuring yourself against your ideal, you measure yourself against where you formerly were.

This may seem counterintuitive. Let me explain.

The story you tell yourself and others is about your future self—your ideal. But when it comes to short-term *measuring of progress,* you want to look back on where you were before. The purpose of measuring the gain regularly is to see the progress you're making. By seeing progress, you feel movement and momentum. This increases your confidence and sense of morale to continue pursuing a future self beyond anything you've been before.

Why is measuring the gain important?

First, it refocuses your "selective attention." We don't see the world objectively but through a subjective lens. That lens is trained based on what we choose to focus on. When you begin focusing on the gains, you train yourself to see progress and momentum. You create a sense of "winning," which boosts your confidence, excitement, and enthusiasm.

That's the purpose and practicality of measuring the gain. It's totally psychological. The goal is to feel great about how you're doing, because these positive emotions and the confidence that comes with them will inspire you to continue pursuing bigger and more challenging goals. Confidence is the foundation of imagination, and it comes from seeing progress.

When you begin proactively framing your narrative, it is incredibly powerful to shift what once was a "gap" narrative to a "gain" one. For example, you may harbor negative emotions about something that happened to you in the past. You may view the experience for all that it cost or has done to you. You may be blaming your current circumstances on those former experiences.

But what would happen if you flipped the script on those experiences? What would happen if you proactively shifted your attention and began looking for the "gains" of such experiences? What would happen if you choose to reframe and retell those stories from an alternative perspective?

History gets revised all the time with new perspectives, experience, and understanding. If your own past hasn't changed, then you're still stuck inside of it. You're not evolving and growing.

Shifting from the gap to the gain is how you *strategically remember* your experiences. It's how you remember your past *intentionally,* not based on your initial emotional reactions but instead on your chosen identity and goals. You are the one who assigns meaning to your experiences. You're the one formulating the story.

So how do you flip your own script?

Re-remembering the past is about filtering your past through the lens of your chosen identity—your future self. How would a more evolved version of you view these events? How have these events enabled you to become who you are today?

Everything in your past has happened—or more accurately, *is happening*—for you, not to you.

Russell Wayne Baker was a highly regarded and famous American journalist, narrator, and author of a Pulitzer Prize–winning autobiography. His autobiography was originally rejected by publishers as "uninteresting." In response to having his story rejected, he told his wife, "I am now going upstairs to invent the story of my life."

The result was the Pulitzer Prize–winning bestseller *Growing Up*.

This "reinvented" version of his own story was no less true than the original version—he simply found a more compelling and useful way to tell that story.

His past, like yours, can be viewed in limitless ways. A terrible experience can be framed as a learning experience. A boring day at school can be framed as a powerful and positive experience.

What you choose to emphasize or ignore in a story determines the focus and impact of the story. Of this, the psychiatrist Gordon Livingston, MD, said, "Each of us have similar latitude in how we interpret our own histories. We have the power to idealize or denigrate those characters that inhabit our life stories. We just need to experience both alternatives as reflections of our current need to see ourselves in certain ways, and to realize that we are all able color our past either happy or sad."

I grew up in a broken home. My parents got divorced when I was eleven. That divorce led my father into a deep depression and ultimately into becoming a drug addict. Throughout my teens, I had very little stability and barely ended up graduating high school. I made a ton of mistakes and faced a lot of emotional pain and confusion.

During this period of my life, I created all sorts of meaning to help me understand and navigate my experiences. Part of that meaning was that my dad had failed me and my younger brothers. He was to blame—the "cause"—for everything wrong in my world.

I felt like a total victim to everything happening *to* me. Almost a year after graduating high school and basically doing nothing with myself, I decided to change my life. I was done playing video games fifteen hours a day. I had always wanted to serve a church mission but had given up on that due to life events and my interpretation of those events.

Pivotal to changing my life was rekindling my relationship with my dad. He had reached out with countless attempts during my high school years. I had shut him out. But in order to move forward and change my life, I knew I needed to begin talking to him again. He and I began meeting for lunches once a week. He encouraged me to serve my mission.

It was approximately ten years ago that I began talking to my dad again and preparing for that church mission. Over those past ten years, I've become an entirely new person. I've learned to look at my past differently—to see the gains rather than the gaps. Like Tucker Max, I view my past with increasing compassion, not judgment. I also view my parents with compassion and understanding instead of judgment.

Part of shifting from the gap to the gain is *getting more information*. On multiple occasions since returning from my mission experience, I've talked to my dad about that difficult period of our lives. He's since cleaned up his life and even spent a few years as an addiction recovery counselor.

In hearing about my teen years *from my dad's perspective*, I've been humbled. He was going through a great deal of trauma himself.

Not only did his divorce shatter him, but his kids abandoned him in his ultimate time of need. I'm not justifying his behavior. But I am choosing *how* I remember my experiences. I'm choosing, based on my current context and perspective, to frame my past based on the gains, not the gaps.

My story used to be about how my father had failed me and my brothers. During my mission experience, my story began to shift. When recounting my past as a missionary, I would explain that I had forgiven my dad for what he had done to us and that the past was "behind me."

But "behind me" wasn't enough. My father was adopted as an infant. I am now the father of three adopted children. Helping my kids through their traumas has helped me rewrite the story of my dad. I'm now seeing my father with increased compassion and understanding.

The meaning of my father's behaviors, and the overall context of that episode, continues to change for me. It's less painful but increasingly pivotal to the growth I've had and continue to experience. In fact, at this point, it is no longer painful to think about or discuss. Everything during that period happened for me, not to me.

Over the past ten years, I've watched my dad change his life in absolutely incredible ways, get himself under control, and become one of my best friends. He is one of my absolute heroes. What he's been able to overcome is truly mind-blowing. So now my narrative about the whole experience is "awe" for what my father went through and for who he became as a result. The transformation and gains are far more meaningful than drilling down and fixating on the specifics of what occurred all those years ago.

The more emotionally developed I become, the less negatively impacted I am by my past and the more I get to shape the meaning of it.

The same is true for you.

At this point, it is your job to reshape your past narrative. The first step is shifting from the gap to the gain. Here's how to do it.

STEP ONE: SHIFT PAST MEANINGS FROM "GAP" TO "GAIN"

Let's practice training your mindset to shift from the gaps to the gains. In order to do so, pull out your journal and answer the following questions:

> Over the past ten years, what significant "wins" or "growth" have you experienced?
>
> How have you, as a person, changed?
>
> What negative things have you let go of?
>
> How have your views of yourself and life changed over the past few years?
>
> What are one to three accomplishments or signs of progress you've had in the past ninety days?

By focusing on the progress, you allow yourself to focus on change and growth. This will enhance your imagination and confidence as you begin to shape your future identity. If you do this consistently, you will train your brain and selective attention to only see growth. You'll train your identity to be positive.

STEP TWO: THINK ABOUT ONE TO THREE NEGATIVE EXPERIENCES FROM YOUR PAST

Now that you've thought about your past in terms of the gain, think about one to three key experiences you feel have negatively impacted your life. Write those experiences down in your journal.

STEP THREE: LIST ALL OF THE BENEFITS OR "GAINS" FROM THOSE ONE TO THREE EXPERIENCES

Now spend some time thinking about and then listing all of the benefits, opportunities, or lessons that have come from those one to three experiences. How have those experiences happened for you, instead of to you?

STEP FOUR: HAVE A CONVERSATION BETWEEN YOUR FUTURE SELF AND YOUR FORMER SELF

Your former self is not gone. They are alive and well. You carry them around with you wherever you go, just as you carry your future self with you wherever you go. However, you're probably carrying around a bruised and broken version of your former self, which is greatly limiting your current and future selves.

It's time to heal and change your former self. You're going to change the meaning of the past. You're going to let go of the pain you've been carrying. You're going to be left with a different identity of your former self. Your former self will now be totally healed.

Measuring the gains of your experiences to see how far you've come is one powerful way of seeing the strengths, rather than the weaknesses, of your former self. Another powerful technique is having a conversation between your future and former selves. You can do this in your journal, your imagination, in a therapy session, however you want.

First, imagine your ideal future self. They are incredibly compassionate, wise, and understanding. They've been through a lot and have created the freedom and capacity you want in your life. To get you started, here are a few questions you could pose in your journal:

How does your future self see your former self?

What would your future self say to your former self?

What experiences would they have, if they were to spend an afternoon together?

What would your former self think of your future self?

How would your former self feel when they heard the loving counsel of your future self?

Who would your former self be after that conversation, once compassionately given permission to let go and move on?

STEP FIVE: CHANGE THE IDENTITY NARRATIVE OF YOUR FORMER SELF

When you shift your story, you see new possibilities for yourself. You're no longer the victim of what happened. Instead, you're the shaper of the meaning of your own experience. Your past is a meaning, a story, which you reconstruct and design here and now.

Every time you go back to your past, you change it.

When healed and healthy, the past is simply a source of information that you can use (not emotion, except for positive and chosen emotions). The past is just raw material to work with. It's entirely malleable and flexible. You get to take the pieces and choose which ones to discard and how you're going to frame them.

Every time you retrieve a memory, you change the memory. The more times you retrieve a memory, the more it will change. Memory is like the telephone game—the more times you tell or imagine the story, the more that story will change. As the neuroscientist Dr. Donna Bridge said, "A memory is not simply an image produced by time traveling back to the original event—it can be an image that is somewhat distorted because of the prior times you remembered it. . . . Your memory of an event can grow less precise even to the point of being totally false with each retrieval."

Following the conversation between your future and former selves, who is your former self now?

> Who is the past version of you that you're now carrying with you?
>
> What is different about your former self now that they've been healed and transformed?
>
> How do you feel about your former self?
>
> When asked about the past, what is the new story you will tell?

As you move forward and change your memories, do so intentionally. Avoid recalling difficult memories when depressed or feeling unsafe. Rather, intentionally visit your memories when you're safe, happy, lighthearted, and with those you know love you.

In a study done by Dr. Bridge, participants were tested on their ability to recall information by looking at a bunch of items on a grid. It was a three-day study. On the first day, the participants saw 180 separate and unique items in various places on the grid. On day two, only some of those 180 items were on the grid, but they were all in a central location. On day three, the participants were tested to see if they could recall which items were on the grid among a large list of random items, and they were also tested on where those items were originally located.

The results showed improved recall accuracy on the final test for objects that were present on day two compared to those not present on day two. However, people never recalled exactly the right location. Instead, they tended to place the object closer to the incorrect location they recalled during day two rather than the correct location from day one.

Their day-two experience altered their memory of their day-one experience. Memories are altered as you retrieve them. As Bridge explains, "Our findings show that incorrect recollection of the object's location on day two influenced how people remembered the object's location on day three. . . . Retrieving the memory didn't simply reinforce the original association. Rather, it altered memory storage to reinforce the location that was recalled at session two."

Every time you look at or view anything, you change it. In physics, a concept known as the *observer effect* shows that the mere observation of a phenomenon inevitably changes that phenomenon. For instance, by simply checking the pressure in an automobile tire, you will inevitably let out at least a small amount of air, and thus change the pressure. Viewing any object places light on that object, causing it to reflect back that light. Even if small, a change will have occurred.

By looking at your past, you will change your past. Every time you look at your past it will change. Every time you look at yourself in the mirror, *you will change.*

A great example of someone who strategically applied the observer effect is Kamal Ravikant, who every time he looked in the mirror would tell himself, "I love you." Since he was struggling with depression, this was initially hard for him to believe. But each time he did this, he changed, even if imperceptibly.

As he repeated these intentional observations thousands of times, he slowly went from depressed and suicidal to purely loving himself. Over time, the person looking back at him from the mirror changed. He now has a totally new personality with a new emotional foundation. His whole story changed—past, present, future.

Regardless of what happened to you in the past, no matter how unique, terrible (or wonderful) it was, you have the same ability to shape who you were and who you will become.

I'm not trying to diminish what happened to you. Nor am I trying to ignore the emotional impact of your previous experiences.

What I'm showing you is that, quite literally, you are the designer of your past. How you *choose to remember* your past is what determines your past far more than what actually happened.

What is your story?

What are the pivotal experiences from your past?

What are the gains you've had from those experiences?

Who was your former self?

How do you feel about your former self?

Who are you now?

Who is your future self?

Your Future Is Fiction: What's It Gonna Be?!

> What we call the beginning is often the end. And to make an end is to make a beginning. The end is where we begin from.
>
> —*T. S. Eliot*

Nate Lambert has always struggled with his weight—as indeed does his whole family. After countless failed attempts to diet and lose weight, Nate conceded that his lot in life was to be overweight and unhealthy. He determined to compensate by succeeding in other areas.

This was hard for him, though, because he saw his parents dealing with extreme health problems. They had all sorts of diseases and limitations due to being overweight. Thinking about this, Nate began to imagine his own future:

What will my future be like if I continue to struggle with my weight? At age seventy, what will I be like?

With his current story and identity, he imagined a future self that was completely unhealthy and unable to do the things he loved, like go on long hikes or travel the world. He also thought about his five kids and his future grandkids. At age seventy, he wouldn't be able to fully enjoy those relationships. If he took the same route as his parents, he'd be completely overweight, unable to move much, and would have all sorts of debilitating diseases.

This vision of his future, and the painful emotions it conjured, was a tipping point for Nate. He determined that a *single decision* he could make, which would make the biggest impact on his health, would be to entirely eliminate refined sugar from his diet *for the rest of his life.*

If he eliminated unhealthy sugars from his diet for the remainder of his life, he could see himself getting his weight under control. He could see himself in his seventies, totally fit and healthy, able to go on hikes and play with his future grandkids. That was a future self he authentically wanted.

That vision for his future self gave Nate a reason to change his identity and behavior. By making that single decision, he would no longer need to obsess and stress about his weight.

In psychology, "decision fatigue" is one way in which our willpower gets exhausted, using up our mental resources to weigh the pros and cons of every decision as we encounter them.

Decision fatigue can be avoided by making a committed choice. For instance, because Nate decided he was going to be sugar-free for life, he no longer had to decide in various situations whether or not he was going to eat sugar. The decision had already been made, and thus decision fatigue—weighing the options and potential outcomes— was no longer a problem.

By not making a clear decision for yourself *beforehand,* you've deferred the decision-making process to some future moment when you're forced to decide.

For instance, when your alarm goes off at five a.m., if you haven't already committed to the decision to get out of bed, you've set yourself up for failure. You've put yourself in a position to make the decision *in that moment*—when you're lying in bed, foggy and exhausted. Instead, keep your alarm across the room where you no longer have a choice. You have to get up and turn it off.

Unknowns are *really* bad for willpower, and ultimately lead people to the negative influences in their environment. You need to know what you'll do in a given situation. The decision needs to be made before you get there, otherwise you become inconsistent, constantly going back and forth with yourself.

The opposite of decision fatigue is making a committed decision. As the basketball legend Michael Jordan is credited for saying, "Once I made a decision, I never thought about it again."

Think about Ken, the man who "never" smoked. Once he decided he'd never smoke again, it wasn't long before he *never thought about smoking again*. Decision fatigue is integral to addiction. The addiction exists because the decision to stop has yet to be made, and thus the mind continues to be consumed.

Harvard business professor Clayton Christensen has said, "It's easier to hold to your principles 100 percent of the time than it is to hold to them 98 percent of the time."

When you're only 98 percent committed to something, then *you haven't truly decided*. As a result, you're required to continue making decisions in every future situation you're in, weighing in every instance whether this particular situation falls into the 2 percent of exceptions you've allowed yourself. In every situation you're in, you're not actually sure what the outcome will be in terms of your behavior and decision-making.

This lack of decision leads to identity confusion and a lack of success. Becoming 100 percent committed to what you want is how you succeed. Making serious and sometimes hard decisions, rather than deferring them for bad situations, leads to enhanced confidence and progress.

Once Nate committed to his decision to cut out refined sugar, his entire identity changed. His new future self—a totally healthy person later in life who could play with his grandkids, travel, and hike— was now shaping his current identity and choices.

It's important to note that "sugar" in itself isn't necessarily the problem. The problem is Nate's imagined future *with sugar*, versus his imagined future without it. If he imagines his future without it, he sees all sorts of possibilities that aren't there when with it.

You can and should do this for yourself. Think about one thing in your life that you aren't entirely aligned with. What would your future be like without that thing in your life?

It's not that the "thing"—whether it is sugar, video games, or any other "vice" or distraction—is inherently "bad" but rather that your future self is different without it.

Decisions shape your future.

Your future shapes your identity.

Your identity shapes your choices and ultimately your personality.

With his new future self in mind, enabled by the decision to go 100 percent refined sugar free for life, Nate began to take an extreme interest in his health. He began reading health books. He researched all of the negative side effects of sugar. He wrote down a list of all of the diseases associated with sugar, such as dementia.

Nate proactively changed his identity *to match his decision.*

Every morning, he declared his daily affirmation that he was a healthy, vibrant, and sugar-free individual. When invited to eat sugary or unhealthy foods, he would affirm his identity by replying, "No, thanks. I'm sugar-free."

In the six months that followed, Nate lost over fifty pounds and his confidence and vision for his future exploded.

Nate's narrative about himself and his past also changed. His story became far more focused on *where he is going* rather than where he was. Nate is not the former fat guy. Instead, he is the healthy and vibrant person he wants to be.

Now it's your turn.

STEP ONE: HONESTLY EXAMINE THE FUTURE YOU'VE CONSIGNED YOURSELF TO

Before imagining your *desired* future self, take some time to honestly think about the future you've currently consigned yourself to have. Remember, Nate had resigned himself to the fact that his future self would be limited, like his parents.

It wasn't until he made the one crucial decision that his desired future self not only became possible but believable.

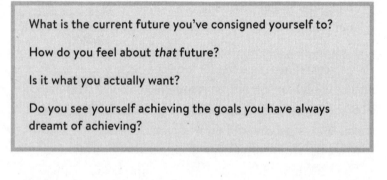

What is the current future you've consigned yourself to?

How do you feel about *that* future?

Is it what you actually want?

Do you see yourself achieving the goals you have always dreamt of achieving?

If you are not completely excited about the future you honestly see unfolding before you, then there's a problem. That limited future self is also limiting who you are now. Your future and your goals are what frame your identity. Thus, with a limited future self, your current identity and behaviors are also going to be less than what they could be. As Dan Sullivan says, "The bigger your future the better your present."

In order to upgrade your identity, actions, and behavior, you need a new future self. You need something you deeply resonate with and are excited about. Something extremely purposeful that you can shape your current identity around.

STEP TWO: WRITE YOUR
OWN BIOGRAPHY

> You need to aim beyond what you are capable of. You need
> to develop a complete disregard for where your abilities end.
> If you think you're unable to work for the best company in its
> sphere, make that your aim. If you think you're unable to be
> on the cover of *Time* magazine, make it your business to be
> there. Make your vision of where you want to be a reality.
> Nothing is impossible.
>
> —*Paul Arden*

You get to write your own story. Pull out your journal and begin your
own biography, as though you were recounting the life of someone
who was no longer alive.

What was your story?

What were the significant events that happened?

How will you be remembered?

How did you live your life?

What did you accomplish?

Take some time to sketch out your own biography. Write from
when you were born up until the present. Then, write from the present through the rest of your life. Every year or so, do this exercise

again. You'll notice that your past and future narrations will change and evolve as you change and evolve. However, the more you do this exercise, the more intentional and creative you'll be in narrating your story.

You'll become increasingly better at creating and living out the story of your imagination. Because you'll be living with greater intention, you'll be having peak experiences more regularly. These peak experiences will alter your perspective and increase your confidence, enabling you to have a more flexible identity. The more flexible you become, the less rigid you'll be about your past and who you think you are. You'll be able to imagine a future self and quickly embody that self.

STEP THREE: IMAGINE YOUR FUTURE SELF THREE YEARS OUT

Who do you want to be three years from now? Get specific.

How much money are you making?

Who are your friends?

What does your typical day look like?

What types of clothes do you wear?

What does your hair look like?

What type of work are you doing?

What does your environment look like?

If you haven't done a lot of future-casting, then you might just start with ninety days from now.

> Who do you want to be in ninety days?
>
> What do you want to have accomplished by then?
>
> How do you want to be different?
>
> What changes do you want to make in your environment?

Instead of just answering these questions in your head, it's far more powerful to write or type them into a "vision" or "future self" statement. This document could be typed and printed and include inspiring pictures that reflect your future self and future circumstances. Examples of pictures could include:

- Pictures with you and your family that you love
- Pictures of people who are physically fit in the way you want to be
- Pictures of environments you want to have, such as a beautiful home
- Pictures of spiritual figures, such as Christ or Buddha, whom you want to emulate
- Pictures of experiences you plan to have, such as a marathon or a trip to a foreign country

This document could be as long as you want, but it also helps to keep it brief and focused.

STEP FOUR: TELL EVERYONE YOUR
NEW STORY . . . *YOUR FUTURE SELF*

> Never mind searching for who you are. Search for the person
> you aspire to be.
>
> —*Robert Brault*

Most people's identity narrative is rooted in their past. From now on, your identity narrative—your "story"—is based on your future self. That's the story you tell people from now on when they ask who you are.

In the musical *Hamilton*, the song "Satisfied" depicts the party where Alexander Hamilton meets the Schuyler sisters, and ultimately, he marries one. Hamilton first meets Angelica. The usual questions arise, focusing on status and class.

> *"My name is Angelica Schuyler."*
> *"Alexander Hamilton."*
> *"Where's your family from?"*
> *"Unimportant. There's a million things I haven't done but just you wait, just you wait . . ."*

Alexander didn't have an amazing past. He didn't have incredible circumstances. He wasn't rich. But he had dreams. His narrative wasn't based on where he currently was or what he had formerly done. His identity narrative was based on what he would do.

Cameron Herold is the founder of the COO Alliance and has helped hundreds of organizations develop what he calls a "Vivid Vision." Herold recommends that organizations keep these Vision documents three to five pages in length and, once developed, to publicize them *everywhere*.

If you're a company, you want everyone on your team to know your vision (not your personality type). You also want all of your clients and prospects to know your vision.

As it relates to yourself, having a three- to five-page printed document of your future self will help you more fully see and believe it. Moreover, you want to share your Vivid Vision document with everyone you know. As you share your vision and goals with those in your life, they will start to hold you more accountable.

Your vision needs to be something that is way above your current reality. It needs to inspire and excite you. It needs to give you motivation and hope. It needs to be something that will stretch and change you. It needs to be big enough that when you look back, you'll be shocked by where and who you currently are.

Your "future self" and "vision" are things that are under constant revision and should be *working documents*. In order for it to be strategic and useful, it's helpful to narrow that vision to three or less years out into the future. The vision should focus on your one major goal, which if you achieve will make your future self and everything else you want in your life possible.

Conclusion

Now that you've reframed your past and imagined your ideal future, it's time to get busy.

It's time to act.

In order to solidify your new identity, you need to begin acting in alignment with that new identity, rather than acting in alignment with your former self. Psychologists have a term for this—*self-signaling,* which means that our actions signal back to us who we are. We judge and measure ourselves by our actions. If you change your behavior, your identity will begin to follow suit.

As you begin acting as your future self, you will eventually become that future self. Your personality will adapt itself to your goals, and you'll have the characteristics, attributes, and circumstances you want.

In order to do so, you must make your future self the new standard for your daily behavior. You must say no to current-self opportunities and options and forgo them for future-self ones.

Your future self is the new standard.

For example, if you are a public speaker and your speaking fee is $5,000, raise your speaking fee to $15,000 and say no if someone won't pay it. Prefer being rejected at your new standard than being accepted at your old one.

Over time, your subconscious catches up to your courage, becoming your new normal. Eventually, the new standard will be replaced with a higher and different one—and not just in monetary terms. Sometimes, the new standard is a lateral rather than vertical upgrade. Make your future self the new standard for your current mindset and behavior.

The next chapter will show you exactly what you need to know.

CHAPTER 5

Enhance Your Subconscious

> The unconscious is the repository of all of our feelings, regardless of their social or personal acceptability. To know about the unconscious is extremely important, for what goes on down there may be responsible for those personality characteristics that drive us to behave as we do.
>
> —Dr. John E. Sarno

In the summer of 1996, Jane Christiansen went waterskiing for her first and only time. Although incredibly healthy and fit, the thirty-six-year-old Jane was also inexperienced. When another boat came too close, creating waves under Jane's skis, she didn't think to let go.

Before she knew it, she was airborne with her right leg thrown awkwardly over the back of her head. When she hit the water, the pain was unbearable. She couldn't move and needed help getting out of the water. The pain was paralyzing.

When she went to the doctor, she learned that her hamstring was 90 percent disconnected from her glutes, almost completely torn off. The doctor told her she'd never be able to run again. This was incredibly devastating, given that Jane led an active lifestyle and had run a marathon just a few months earlier. Although it was a bitter pill to swallow, she took the doctor's words as gospel and resigned herself to never running again. A premature cognitive commitment was rooted.

Still, in the aftermath of the accident, Jane recovered quickly and resumed her normal, healthy, and active lifestyle—albeit without running. She avoided facing the trauma, and her fixed mindset regarding her ability to run solidified.

Fast forward to 2011: Jane's husband surprisingly lost what they thought to be a secure job. Instead of looking for new employment, he decided to take an early retirement. This was a shock to Jane, and infuriating. She worked hard running a business and didn't like seeing her husband spending his day on the golf course. But she kept this to herself as she didn't want to hurt his feelings or be viewed by others as a complainer.

So she bottled up her growing rage.

Then something happened that didn't make immediate sense. The pain in her right hamstring came back, and it was just as excruciating as when the waterskiing accident occurred *fifteen years prior*. Not only that, but her left foot also began to throb. The pain was out of nowhere, unexplainable, and intense.

How did this happen?

Jane went to see a doctor. His explanation was that she was now over fifty years old and her leg pain was part of the *natural process of aging*. He diagnosed her with tendonitis and arthritis. It didn't make sense to Jane, but just as she had done fifteen years earlier, she accepted the doctor's diagnosis.

I guess I'm just getting older, was the narrative that formulated in Jane's mind, born out of a cognitive commitment she had accepted, which eventually turned into her biological reality.

Subsequently, the pain only got worse. Her fitness became increasingly limited. During the hiking season of 2011, she didn't hike a single time despite it being her favorite pastime. Her pain affected her work as well.

Meanwhile, her rage and frustration toward her husband festered quietly. Sometimes she was so angry she couldn't even walk. All the while, she never told anyone about the pain she was experiencing. Being the owner of a health business, and someone whom others saw as a beacon of health and positivity, she wanted to maintain her appearance.

She was a perfectionist, and had been one since she was a little girl. She didn't want anyone to think she was struggling.

Fast forward to 2014: Jane attended a business and marketing event. At that event, she was introduced to Joe Polish, the founder of Genius Network and Genius Recovery. When Joe saw Jane walk up with a limp, he asked her about it.

"What's going on with you?" he said, motioning to her leg.

Jane brushed it off. "Oh, nothing, just some leg pain."

"What do you mean 'leg pain'? Did you have an injury or something?"

"Yeah, I was in a waterskiing accident and I'm over fifty now."

"Was this accident recent?"

"No, it was almost twenty years ago."

"Wait, you're experiencing pain from something twenty years ago?"

"I guess so, I don't really know," Jane replied.

Joe then connected Jane to a friend, Steven Ozanich, who is an expert on the connection between suppressed emotions and physical pain.

A few days later, Jane was on the phone with Steven. He didn't ask her anything about her physical symptoms, or if she was seeing any doctors, or doing any kind of physical therapy to fix the problem. Instead, he just asked her a bunch of questions about her life.

"Are you married?"

"Yes."

"What does your husband do for work?"

"Well, he's not employed. He lost his job three years ago."

"How does that make you feel?"

"It's actually really hard to deal with."

"No, I asked you how does this make you *feel*?" Steven pushed.

Jane continued to fumble about her emotions. "It's difficult."

"No. Seriously. How does your husband being unemployed make you feel?"

"It makes me feel upset."

"Just upset?"

"To be completely honest with you, it really pisses me off."

"It sounds like you're really angry about this."

"I am. Sometimes I feel a lot of anger."

"When did the pain in your legs start?"

"About three years ago, right around when my husband lost his job."

"All right, here's what's happening," Steven said. "Your pain has absolutely nothing to do with your waterskiing injury. Your pain is stemming from the emotions you have toward your husband. You need to find a way to express your emotions."

That's basically where their first conversation ended. He told her to read his book *The Great Pain Deception*, and after she did so, they could have another conversation.

After the phone call, Jane immediately bought the book, but when it arrived in the mail, she didn't read it. Although the conversation with Steven had been interesting, it didn't resonate with her. She couldn't accept the idea that her suppressed emotions were the real cause of her problems.

Several months later, in February 2015, Jane got an email from Steven:

"Hey, Jane, how are you doing?"

"I'm good, but I'm still in pain. I haven't read your book yet but I promise I will."

Immediately after sending the email, she grabbed Steven's book off her bookshelf and read the whole thing that week. By the time she finished it, the pain in both of her legs felt 90 percent gone. She emailed Steven back excitedly and scheduled another call. He explained that her pain was gone because of "knowledge therapy," which made her aware of the true cause of her pain and problems.

During a second call, Steven asked what Jane had been doing about the pain over the past several years, and what she was currently doing.

She had done all sorts of expensive therapies and treatments, even flying across the country to try experimental therapies. Steven told her to stop everything she was doing to treat the pain. No more acupuncture, massage, chiropractic, and so on.

"Stop all of that stuff," he told her. "It fuels the belief that this is a physical problem. Carry on with life as if everything was normal. If you're working out and you start to feel the pain, just keep exercising. Push through as though the pain wasn't happening. In addition to stopping all of the physical treatments, you need to start expressing your emotions."

From that moment forward, Jane made four shifts:

1. She immediately stopped all of the physical therapies she was doing, which she was spending tens of thousands of dollars on.
2. She also started what she calls her "Rage Journal," where she expresses all of her frustration and anger.
3. She started talking to her husband about how she was feeling.
4. *She also started running again.*

With these four behavioral shifts, Jane's entire life changed. She realized that to stay pain-free, she needed to express her emotions as they occurred. She couldn't bottle up and suppress them anymore. Being able to run again also built her confidence.

Fast forward to 2019: Jane is fifty-eight years old and more active and healthier than she's ever been since the accident. She hasn't had pain in her legs for over four years. People around her are shocked as she seems to look younger every year. She continues to push people to the limit in the fitness classes she teaches. Her radiance glows in brightness.

Jane is a lot more understanding about her past. She isn't as judgmental toward her husband, and sees how she's created stress in the marriage over the years as well. She sees herself dying very old and completely healthy, fit, and pain-free. She also sees herself happily married to her husband for the remainder of their lives, something she hadn't been sure of over her last several years of frustration.

Jane's perfectionism and emotional rigidity have been replaced with increased psychological flexibility. She used to get frustrated and angry about any messes or disorganization in their home. She is now more flexible in her personal relationships.

"Some things just really don't matter, like if the bed isn't made."

And while she maintains her high standards at work, she's even noticed herself becoming more open too, allowing her employees to execute their own ideas without having to do things her way.

Jane is in far greater touch with her emotions now. When she notices herself being triggered, or when she feels stressed or anxious due to work demands or something going on in her relationships, she immediately gives herself space and pulls out her journal to process her thoughts. She never goes anywhere without her Rage Journal.

Before expressing her thoughts and feelings with others, she processes and organizes them first in her journal. This makes communication clearer and based more on her chosen secondary emotions rather than her initial reaction or state. Journaling and connecting with herself helps her avoid making premature cognitive commitments during emotionally difficult situations. It allows her to reconnect with her future self and the life she wants to create.

She's learned to communicate her needs. She sets better boundaries for herself and her relationships. She's less of a people pleaser. Her emotional development and flexibility as a person have evolved, and thus her personality has changed. She's less rigid and stuck in the past. She's more in touch with the present, more connected to others, and pulled forward by her future self.

Jane's story is her own, and is one of many. People experience pain for different reasons, and while I am not qualified nor is it my intention to give medical advice, it is alarming how many people experience chronic physical pain for reasons that stem from an underlying psychological trauma.

For the remainder of this chapter, I'm going to break down a great deal of science exploring the connection between our emotions, our subconscious, and our physical body. It's important to keep in mind that while the science describes general trends in the population, each person's situation is unique, and so none of this should be taken as medical advice.

Your Memories Are Physical, and Your Body Is Emotional

Although we tend to think of our memories as abstract and mental, they are *physical and physiological*. Your physical body is the evidence of your past—the embodied memory of everything that has come before. Or as Bessel van der Kolk, MD, put it in the very title of his book: *The Body Keeps the Score.*

The experiences in our lives become our biology. Those experiences are memories stored in specific areas of our body. In the case of Jane, her waterskiing trauma created a memory that was stored in her leg. As Dr. Steven Cole, the director of the UCLA Social Genomics Core Laboratory, has said, "A cell is a machine for turning experience into biology."

Jane's story highlights the fundamental connection between our emotions and our physical body. Although rarely connected by any medical professional, in reality, they are one in the same.

The glue that holds our body, memories, and identity together is our emotions.

Like memory, we tend to think of emotions as abstract, residing only in our minds. They are not. *Emotions are physical.*

That bears repeating. Emotions and memories have physical markers in your body. According to the molecular biologist and neuroscientist Dr. Candice Pert, the surfaces of every cell throughout our body are lined with "receptors" that receive messages through neuro-peptides, which are small protein molecules that relay information throughout our body and brain. Dr. Pert calls these peptides the "molecules of emotion," explaining that the information relayed and stored throughout our brain and body is *emotions*.

In other words, the information relayed throughout the brain and body are emotional in nature. That information—the emotional content—then *becomes the body*.

The experiences we have transform not only our perspectives and identity but become our very biology.

Why does this matter? Because we need to reframe how we see our body, *and look at it as an emotional system*. Emotions are chemical, and our body becomes accustomed or habituated to these chemicals. Take dopamine, for example. Your body becomes habituated to a certain dosage of dopamine, and when the chemical levels are low, the body literally *needs* more. As a result, and without conscious thought, your hand reaches for your smartphone, and you go through a subconscious loop you've played out repeatedly in the past.

We catch ourselves doing this all the time.

We do various things out of habit or addiction. The reason we subconsciously engage in repetitious behaviors is because our body has become addicted to the emotions that our behaviors create. The emotion is a chemical relayed and released throughout the body, recreating the homeostasis that is the physical body.

This is why overcoming an addiction is so difficult. Addiction isn't merely a mental disorder. It is physical. In order to change your addiction, you literally need to change your biology. You need a future self with a new identity, a new story, new environment, and new body.

What chemicals are you addicted to?

What emotions does your body thrive on and continuously reproduce?

Many people are addicted to the chemical cortisol, which is stress. If they aren't feeling stressed, they get uneasy and do things to create more stress in their lives.

In his book *The Big Leap*, Dr. Gay Hendricks explains that when people begin a journey of personal transformation, they will subconsciously sabotage themselves in order to get back to their accustomed level: "Each of us has an inner thermostat setting that determines how much love, success, and creativity we allow ourselves to enjoy. When we exceed our inner thermostat setting, we will often do something to sabotage ourselves, causing us to drop back into the old, familiar zone where we feel secure."

Dr. Hendricks calls this the "Upper Limit Problem." When you begin making improvements in your life, you're going to subconsciously try to get back to where you feel comfortable. This is emotional.

If you're not used to feeling amazing all the time, then when you start allowing yourself to feel good, your subconscious will grow uneasy. It wants negative emotions because negative chemicals are what literally make up your body.

I've seen this happen in my own life. In fact, it happened big-time while I was writing this book. Over the past few years, I've made huge leaps in terms of my education, finances, network, family, and overall happiness. However, over the past year, I almost threw everything away.

I noticed myself trying to subconsciously sabotage everything amazing in my life. I got addicted to caffeine, travel, and confusion.

I couldn't get myself to write. I wasted huge amounts of time watching YouTube videos. I had a hard time getting motivated.

As I watched myself beginning to struggle, I could see what was happening. Once I noticed that I was damaging myself, I realized that I needed to seek help. I started by expressing to my wife and others that I was on a downward spiral. We began therapy, set new goals, and made important adjustments to our family and routines.

I re-created my future self. I got my vision going again. Without a clear vision pulling us forward, life becomes about how much willpower you are able to summon every day. What I needed was a goal to direct my identity and behavior. I needed a target.

I used my future self as the filter for setting firmer boundaries in my life. This involved having hard conversations with people I deeply cared about, telling them I needed to readjust our relationship and put my priorities—like my faith, family, and health—back at the forefront. I was humbled as most of these people were respectful and supportive, even if slightly frustrated, such as when business plans were required to change or when I canceled scheduled speaking engagements.

All of these conversations, adjustments in purpose, and behaviors were subconscious-enhancing—moving me at the fundamental level closer to my future self, not just conceptually. This was deep work, and deep work is emotional.

If you don't change your subconscious, then altering your personality will be difficult. If you change your subconscious, then altering your personality happens automatically.

To make powerful change in our lives, we need to change at the subconscious level. Otherwise, the change will not be permanent.

You could try to force yourself to be positive, for example, but if your subconscious, or physical body, is habituated to negative emotional states, it will default to behaviors that reproduce those emotions. Willpower doesn't work for overcoming addictions, at least not in an effective or predictable way.

Your body seeks homeostasis by leading you to behaviors and experiences that reproduce the emotional climate it is used to—not necessarily the behaviors that are best for you.

You are an emotional being. Your physical body is your "subconscious mind," and the only way to alter your subconscious is by shifting the emotional framework that makes you who you are.

For a time, Jane had become accustomed to anger and rage. Those were the emotions she became addicted to. Her life became a pattern to re-create those emotions, even if consciously she was doing her best to be positive. As a result, those emotions became her biology, manifested through her leg pain.

Dr. John E. Sarno, a former professor of rehabilitation medicine and attending physician at New York University, argues that physical pain, such as back pain, "exists only to distract [the person's] attention away from the emotions. . . . There's nothing like a little physical pain to keep your mind off your emotional problems." Dr. Sarno explains that this is a survival mechanism of the body because it's easier for us to live with physical pain than emotional pain.

In many cases, the cause of physical pain is not "physical" at all but *emotional*. Once a person accepts the fact that they have suppressed emotions, and learns to express and reframe them, they will stop misdiagnosing their pain as a physical condition. Of this, Steven Ozanich wrote in *The Great Pain Deception*, "Pain and other chronic symptoms are physical manifestations of unresolved internal conflict. Symptoms surface as the instinctual mechanism for self-survival. They are messages from the inner self wanting to be heard, but ego takes center stage, and hides the truth within the shadows of the unconscious mind: which is the body."

When you change your subconscious, your personality will change as well. Your personality is merely a by-product or reflection of where you are emotionally. If you maintain suppressed emotions, you'll develop a personality to either cope with or avoid them.

The untransformed trauma (and the fixed mindset it creates) stunts your imagination. Your future self and purpose are then either nonexistent or extremely limited. As a result, you become a version of yourself that is far less than you could have been. You engage in behaviors and situations to produce emotions that numb the pain you're suppressing.

This isn't what you want to do. This isn't who you want to be. Think about yourself for a moment:

Why have you become who you are?

Are you the person you've become out of choice, or out of reaction to your life's experiences?

What would happen if you became the person you really wanted to be?

What would happen if you allowed yourself to feel good more often?

What would happen if you stopped avoiding your pain?

Practice Fasting

> The best of all medicines are rest and fasting.
>
> — *Benjamin Franklin*

Fasting from food for eighteen-plus hours is one of the most powerful ways to enhance your subconscious. Given that your physical body is your subconscious, when you purposefully deprive yourself from food, you are literally resetting the body, allowing it to rest and recover rather than digest.

Fasting has been found to rapidly dissipate the craving for nicotine, alcohol, caffeine, and other drugs. It also increases levels of catecholamines—such as dopamine—which elevates your happiness and confidence while reducing your anxiety. Fasting actually increases your number of brain cells.

Fasting can increase your longevity and lifespan. Research has found that age-related declines in cognitive and motor abilities (such as physical balance) can be reduced by fasting. It also reduces cognitive stressors that bring about aging, cognitive decline, and chronic diseases.

Other research has found that fasting can improve the overall quality of your sleep. It also improves focus, learning, memory, and ability to comprehend information. Research at Yale has found that being on an empty stomach helps you think and focus better. Hence, many people, such as Malcolm Gladwell, purposefully skip breakfast so they can better focus on their creative work.

Many books have been written about the benefits of fasting. However, as it relates to enhancing your subconscious, the point is that fasting can improve confidence, emotional flexibility, and self-control. Fasting is a form of physical and emotional *practice* that enables you to connect to your deeper side.

Personally, I've been practicing fasting consistently for nearly fifteen years. Generally, I'll fast from all foods and liquids for twenty-four hours once or twice per month. Or anytime I feel so inspired. This practice has not only enhanced my spirituality and decision-making ability but my mental clarity and focus as well.

Having a regular fasting practice, if physically able, is a powerful aid to clarifying and becoming your future self. While in a fasted state, you can have greater clarity and intuitive connection. You can visualize and decide who you want to be. If you're trying to make any major or important decisions, consider fasting to get clarity about that decision. From a more spiritual perspective, fasting and prayer go hand in hand. They are powerful at helping you get clear on what you're trying to do, in addition to moving past what has been keeping you stuck.

There are many ways to go about fasting. Fasting from food and caloric beverages for sixteen to twenty-four hours is a great practice for healing and connecting mentally and physically. Also, fasting from technology, particularly the internet, for twenty-four-hour periods of time or more is also incredibly powerful for connecting with yourself and getting clarity.

Once per week, you could take a break from food and the internet. If you did this, you'd be shocked at the clarity and confidence you'd get. Fasting with a specific purpose and intent makes the experience more powerful. Doing anything intentionally makes the activity better and opens the possibility of having peak experiences. I can attest that many times while fasting, I've gotten the very insights I needed to make key decisions or changes in my life. Had I not given myself the space from food and the internet, I wouldn't have gotten that clarity. My life wouldn't be where it's at.

Give Money Away: Make Regular Charitable Donations

> You have to feel that you deserve good things or else your subconscious might very well sabotage all your best efforts. If you don't truly feel that you deserve great financial success, then you are battling an almost insurmountable obstacle: your subconscious. Giving regular gifts from your income to charity is one excellent way of once and for all, persuading your subconscious that you deserve what lies ahead. In this way, it will not only end its sabotage, it will begin actively to assist in your quest.
>
> —*Rabbi Daniel Lapin*

Research using functional magnetic resonance imaging (fMRI) showed that charitable giving was linked with feelings of happiness. Other research supports the idea that altruistic financial behaviors such as gift giving or providing charitable donations are linked to happiness. Research has found that happiness is related to successful outcomes. Thus, engaging in behaviors that make you feel happy is obviously worthwhile.

Although happiness is all well and good, giving money away can and does have a tangible and powerful impact on your subconscious. It sends a powerful signal to yourself that you are the type of person who gives to others. Giving money away is a subconscious-enhancing behavior. You can and should use it as a tool for expanding your identity. For instance, although a religious example, the story of George Cannon highlights how making charitable donations can transform your identity and capacity for love.

George Cannon was a Christian. As part of his faith, he was encouraged to tithe 10 percent of his income, a notion that is repeated throughout the Bible. However, despite being a young and impoverished man, George approached tithing in a very nontraditional, and far more transformative, way.

Rather than paying retroactively, wherein he paid 10 percent of what he earned, he decided to pay 10 percent of what he *intended to earn in his future.* Discussing this story in a talk, mental health scholar and therapist Dr. Wendy Watson Nelson explained, "When his bishop commented on the large amount of tithing poor young George was paying, George said something like, 'Oh bishop, I'm not paying tithing on what I make. I'm paying tithing on what I want to make.' And the very next year George earned exactly the amount of money he had paid tithing on the year before!"

George was not transactional in his approach to tithing. *He was transformational.* He didn't see tithing as a cost, but an investment in his future self and his relationship with God.

George's behavior was subconscious-enhancing. He was seeing, and acting as, his future self, not his present or former self. He was operating from his future circumstances—as though they were already real—rather than operating from his current circumstances.

His financial investment became a forcing function. He put himself, financially and psychologically—even spiritually—in a position where he felt not only inspired but compelled to act in faith. He paid 10 percent of what he wanted to make. When he made that investment, he prayed and acted from the vantage point of someone earning ten times what he had invested.

As a result, George quickly became that person.

I first heard this story in January of 2017. Since then, I've applied charitable giving in a more proactive way. My income has increased dramatically. But more than just an increase in income, my identity and confidence has changed. I believe I have a greater capacity to learn and grow. I'm far more flexible. I have greater trust and faith that things will work out my way. I'm more willing to take courageous leaps.

I also take opportunities to help people in need, when it makes sense. Recently, I was in an Uber and my driver was a single mom of four in her early fifties. She was working sixty-plus hours per week trying to get her kids through college. She wanted to finish her own degree, but was chipping away at various bills that were keeping her stuck. I decided to pay one of the bills, which was a few hundred bucks. To her, this meant she could get back to her schooling a year before she anticipated.

Tears came to her eyes. She was in disbelief. The impact my gift had on her was surprising to me. It humbled me and made me want to increase my financial situation so I could help more people. Thus, this experience expanded my subconscious and my future self.

You too should apply the concept of charitable giving as a technique for enhancing your subconscious. The more you give, the greater will become your capacity to give. As Mark Victor Hansen and Robert Allen explain: "Giving taps into the spiritual dimension that multiplies us, our thinking, and our results. . . . There is an ocean of abundance and one can tap into it with a teaspoon, a bucket, or a tractor trailer. The ocean doesn't care."

Conclusion

In order to become your future self, you must transform yourself at the core and subconscious level. Wishful thinking and rare moments of visualization are not enough. You must engage in behaviors and have peak experiences that shift your identity and create a new sense of "normal" for you. Fasting and charitable giving are just two of many subconscious-enhancing behaviors.

Rather than being defined by your former behaviors, you can and should be defined by your future behaviors. Rather than being defined by experiences from your past, you can and should be defined by the peak experiences you'll create in the future—those experiences that will transform you from who you are into who you plan to be.

CHAPTER 6

Redesign Your Environment

> If I changed the environmental situation, the fate of the cells
> would be altered. I would start off with my same muscle
> precursors but in an altered environment they would actually
> start to form bone cells. If I further altered the conditions,
> those cells became adipose or fat cells. The results of these
> experiments were very exciting because while every one of
> the cells was genetically identical, the fate of the cells was
> controlled by the environment in which I placed them.
>
> —*Bruce Lipton, MD*

In 1979, Harvard psychologist Dr. Ellen Langer and a group of graduate students designed the interior of a building to reflect 1959—twenty years prior. There was a black-and-white TV, old furniture, and magazines and books from the 1950s scattered about. This would be the home to a group of eight men, all in their seventies or eighties, for the next five days.

When these men arrived at the building for the study, they were told they should not merely discuss this past era but *behave as if* they actually were their prior selves, twenty years ago.

"We have good reason to believe that if you are successful at this you will feel as you did in 1959," Langer told them.

From that moment on, the study subjects were treated as if they were in their fifties rather than their seventies. Despite several being stooped over and having to use canes to walk, they were not aided in taking their belongings up the stairs.

"Take them up one shirt at a time if you have to," they were told by the research assistants.

Their days were spent listening to radio shows, watching movies, and discussing sports and other "current events" from the period. They could not bring up any events that happened after 1959 and referred to themselves, their families, and their careers as they were in that year.

The goal of this study was not for these men to live in the past. The goal was to trigger their minds and bodies to exhibit the energy and biological responses of a much younger person.

What happened?

In short, these men got *younger.*

They literally got taller. There was noticeable improvement in their hearing, eyesight, memory, dexterity, and appetite. They gained weight, which for these men was a good thing.

Those who had arrived using canes, and dependent on the help of their children, left the building under their own power and carrying their own suitcases.

By expecting these men to function independently and engaging with them as individuals rather than "old people," Langer and her students gave them "an opportunity to see themselves differently," *which impacted them biologically.*

Context Shapes Roles:
Roles Shape Identity and Biology

How you treat other people influences how they see themselves. How people see themselves influences their mindset and emotions, yes. But it also impacts their biology. This truth has extreme implications. To adapt a quote from Goethe, "The way you see [a child] is the way you treat them and the way you treat them is [who] they [will] become."

As human beings, we generally default to the roles of our social environment. It takes extreme intentionality and decisiveness not to default to an expected social or cultural role.

As men in their seventies and eighties, they probably didn't expect to have to carry their bags by themselves. Their opinions hadn't mattered for many years. They likely forgot what it felt like to be stronger, younger, and more confident. But absorbing themselves in a new context and then acting out the role of that environment transformed them.

Putting yourself in new environments, around new people, and taking on new roles is one of the quickest ways to change your personality, for better or worse. Fully take on the roles you assume, and you'll change from the outside in.

By this point, I hope I have convinced you that your personality is dynamic and ever-changing, largely based on the roles you play and the situations in which you find yourself.

The word "personality" comes from the Latin word *persona*. In the ancient world, a persona was a mask worn by an actor in a theater. It can also mean a character played by an actor. When you put on a different mask or play a different character, you portray a different persona. As William Shakespeare wrote, "All the world's a stage, and all the men and women merely players: they have their exits and their entrances; and one man in his time plays many parts."

Think about this for a minute: *Are you always the same person?*

That may seem like a strange question, because internally, you always feel like you, right?

Or do you?

Do you *really* feel like the same person in all situations and circumstances? Of course not. In some situations, you may be bored, awkward, or shy. In others, you're on top of the world. The "you" that shows up is very different depending on the situation.

If your house was being robbed, you'd be different than if you were sitting on an airplane or at work or at a rock concert. Around certain people, such as old high school friends, you may reflect a younger and less mature version of yourself. Sometimes you're more introverted and sometimes more extroverted.

But here's what's interesting: As a person ages, they tend to stop engaging in new situations, experiences, and environments. In other words, people's personalities become increasingly consistent because they stop putting themselves into new contexts. Indeed, the philosopher and psychologist William James believed that a person's personality basically became fully formed and fixed by age thirty, because thereafter a person's life often becomes highly routine and predictable.

Although the culture is rapidly changing, there are still similar patterns. By the time a person reaches their thirties, they stop having as many "first" experiences. In their childhood, teens, and even twenties, there are a lot of experiences: First kiss. First time driving. First job. First big failure. First time moving to a new city. But at some point, we "settle down." We stop engaging in new roles and new situations that bring out new and different sides of us.

Because people's lives become highly routine, both in their social roles and their environments, you begin to see very predictable behaviors and attitudes. This is one of the core reasons why personality is viewed as stable and predictable over time. It's not that your personality itself becomes stable but rather that your routine environments and social roles lock you into habitual patterns.

According to Stanford psychologist Lee Ross, "We see consistency in everyday life because of the power of the situation." Ross further explains that ultimately it's the situation and not the person that determines how the person consistently shows up. "People are predictable, that's true. . . . But they're predictable because we see them in situations where their behavior is constrained by that situation and the roles they're occupying and the relationships they have with us."

> When was the last time you did something for the first time?
>
> When was the last time you did something unpredictable?
>
> When was the last time you put yourself in a new situation or a new role?
>
> Are there clothes in your closet that have been there for over five years?

Research on the Big Five personality factors—openness, conscientiousness, extraversion, agreeableness, neuroticism—show that as people age, they become increasingly less open to having new experiences. They stop surrounding themselves with new types of people.

They stop engaging in new roles and in new environments. They stop taking on new challenges. They stop experiencing new emotions.

People become old far too fast.

The more psychologically rigid a person is, the more they see themselves as and even attempt to be *the same person in every situation they are in*. This narrow approach lacks recognition that in different situations, not only should you be a different person, but in different situations *you can't help* being a different person.

From a Western perspective, this may not make a lot of sense. Westerners tend to view the world from what is called an "atomistic" viewpoint, which assumes that something (or someone) can be understood regardless of context. Fundamental to this view is isolating and abstracting things from their context and attempting to explain them for their "innate" traits.

This atomistic worldview is why we as a culture obsess about individual characteristics like "habits" and "hacks." It's also why we view personality as fixed and unchanging, and it's why we love our personality tests.

A more accurate and scientific perspective would be to view the world "relationally." From a *relational worldview*, nothing can be understood outside of its context. In fact, it is the context or "relationship between" that *determines the meaning* of the thing.

If you were to lose a person you love, you wouldn't just lose that person but also *the person you were when with them*. All loss includes a loss of yourself. And conversely, meeting new people or entering new relationships leads to the creation of a new self.

The relationship between my wife, Lauren, and me makes each of us who we are. Who Lauren is, from my perspective, is far different from who she is from someone else's perspective. You change Lauren's context, you change Lauren.

Likewise, you as a person can only be understood in context. If you had grown up at a different time and in a different place, *you'd be a different person*. You'd have different memories, connections, and beliefs. If you had lived two thousand years ago in a different culture, you wouldn't be addicted to your cell phone. You'd have different interests in clothing, people, entertainment, and goals.

Undeniably, your personality is shaped by what surrounds you. Culture is often ignored because it seems invisible, but it shapes identity, behavior, relationships, and personality. If you find yourself in consistent environments and consistent social roles, then your personality will show up as stable and consistent over time.

As an example, there is a vast amount of research showing that your peer group powerfully influences your behavior and choices. Specifically, research shows that peer and social groups influence:

- Academic achievement
- Choice of university and degree
- How productive you are at work
- Whether or not you cheat in school and other life domains
- Whether you're likely to do extracurricular activities and go above and beyond the call of duty
- Whether you engage in risky behaviors such as smoking, doing harmful drugs, and using alcohol
- Your likelihood of engaging in criminal behaviors
- The financial decisions you make and how well you ultimately do financially
- Your chances of becoming an entrepreneur

Your social and peer groups shape your identity, how you see yourself, and who you become. You engage in behaviors that match the culture of your group. You come to develop a role and identity within your peer groups. Your peer groups shape the choices you make, the goals you set, and how well you do in life.

When Lauren and I were dating, we spent some time with a particular group of my old high school friends. She saw a side of me she didn't know existed and, frankly, didn't like. Trust me when I say that Lauren and I would never have been high school friends, let alone sweethearts.

With my old friends, I immediately shifted back into the role, identity, behavior, and even language patterns I exhibited in high school. Lauren saw me go from the Ben she had been dating to high school Ben in an instant. All due to a quick change in context and role.

While we were driving home that night, Lauren told me she did not like the Ben she had just seen. She was stunned. It became extremely obvious to both of us that my present and former selves were two very different people, but that the former could return quickly if the role and context facilitated it. I let her know I was committed to my future, not my past.

Not surprisingly, then, research has found that how you score on a personality test is heavily influenced by situational factors. In different cultures, the Big Five personality model doesn't even work the same way as in the Western and American culture where it was developed. People from different cultures view personality differently, and thus respond differently to the test.

What's more, research has shown that the specific conditions the personality test is taken in also dictate the results of the test. In one study, participants were given the same personality test at two different times. Half the participants were given the test by the same person at both times, whereas the other half were given their personality test by two different administrators. According to Dr. Christopher Soto, one of the psychologists running this study, "The most surprising thing to me was if someone was interviewed twice by the same interviewer then their responses across the two tests were pretty consistent. . . . But if they were interviewed by two different interviewers then their responses were often completely unrelated to each other."

You see yourself differently and act differently based on what surrounds you.

The purpose of this chapter is to help you become more strategic about your environment. Until you become intentional and serious about your context, you will never be able to become who you want to be.

Although it is common for people to be the mere products of their environment, you must learn to make your environment match your desired outcomes. When you do, your personality will organically follow suit.

Specifically, this chapter will teach you three fundamental strategies of environmental design:

1. Strategic remembering
2. Strategic ignorance
3. Forcing functions

Strategic Remembering

Consider the apocryphal story of the American artist James Abbott McNeill Whistler, who once painted a small spray of roses. It was admired by many other painters and collectors of the time. Other painters who saw the work were inspired by and envious of it. It seemed as though Whistler had been touched by the hand of God in the creation of that painting.

Collectors yearned to buy the painting. But Whistler refused to sell his finest work. Instead, he kept it near him at all times as a *continuous reminder* of what was possible for him. As he once stated:

> Whenever I feel that my hand has lost its cunning, whenever I doubt my ability, I look at the little picture of the spray of roses and say to myself, "Whistler, you painted that. Your hand drew it. Your imagination conceived the colors. Your skill put the roses on the canvas." I know that what I have done I can do again.

Whistler was strategic about his environment. He was strategic about how he wanted to feel and what he wanted to remember. That piece of art sitting near his work desk served as a continuous reminder of the type of work he wanted to do. It inspired him to see himself from a different perspective. It lifted his spirits when he was depressed or frustrated.

Like Whistler, you need to be strategic about what you remember. You need an environment that continuously calls to mind your future self. If your environment doesn't continuously bring your future self to the forefront, then your environment is activating a different you.

Despite the fact that we sometimes remember our most traumatic experiences for years or decades, for the most part human beings are *incredibly forgetful*. We can forget where we parked our car. We can forget that we promised our child we would take them to get doughnuts in the morning.

We can forget what we truly want in our lives. Life gets busy and sometimes the routine of keeping up with the bills can take over. As

Meredith Willson wrote in the Broadway hit *The Music Man,* "You pile up enough tomorrows, and you'll find you are left with nothing but a lot of empty yesterdays."

James Whistler was not the only one to design his environment for strategic remembering. The author and podcaster Tim Ferriss keeps a copy of the book *The Magic of Thinking Big* facing outward on his bookshelf. Tim read that book at a formative time and it changed his life. Consequently, the book now serves as a trigger for thinking and "playing" bigger for him. All he has to do is see the cover and he experiences an immediate shift in mindset, emotion, and identity.

A memento can also be used to warn or remind you of what matters. Author Ryan Holiday has a coin he keeps in his pocket that says on it *Memento Mori,* translated as "Remember Death." Holiday keeps this coin on him to trigger feelings of his own mortality, which keep him focused on his priorities rather than being distracted.

To strategically remember and live the identity I most want, I recently had a "Culture Wall" created by the culture design company Gapingvoid. A Culture Wall is a collection of twelve or more of your most important beliefs or aspirations that are then illustrated as individual artworks installed on a wall in a grid format. Culture Walls are immersive symbols that become a "shrine of ideas."

My Culture Wall, which I had installed in my home, displays many of my highest ideals, which I want not only myself but also my children to be continuously reminded of. It's fun to see my kids repeating phrases from the Culture Wall they see several times every day in our home. I hear them say things like:

"Do what is right, let the consequences follow."
"Better prolific than perfect."

"You make or break your life before eight a.m."

"100 percent is easier than 98 percent."

"Expect everything and attach to nothing."

"The measure of intelligence is the ability to change."

"Assume the feeling of your wish fulfilled."

"You can't be free without uncertainty."

"What got you here won't get you there."

"Never be the former anything."

"Embrace your future to change your past."

"Gratitude changes things."

"Good timber does not grow with ease."

"Nothing happens until after the boats are burned."

These are the beliefs I want to instill in myself and my kids. Every time I walk by my Culture Wall while heading upstairs, I look at the images and am reminded of the person I want to be, which I can sometimes forget to be in the busyness of life.

Your environment should be full of strategic reminders of who you want to be, helping you to become your desired future self.

For Whistler, the picture of his roses was more than just a picture of roses. It became a symbol to him of deep meaning and significance. He could look at that picture, and his identity and emotions would immediately be changed. He could go from lacking confidence to being activated and capable. In a quick blink, he felt the power of his future and goals. His emotions were changed and he could create art from a more empowered identity.

That's the power of strategic remembering.

If you're going to create a life of meaning and growth, you need to proactively design your environment with *transformational triggers*. This is opposite of how most environments are designed. Most environments are filled with negative triggers that create undesirable and unresolved emotions.

Instead, you want to create triggers that click you into your future, not your former, self. Think of it: You've strategically designed your environment to remind you of your future. Remembering doesn't need to only be about the past.

Open your eyes and look at the environment you have created around you. Are you still hanging on to concert posters from college? Do the artwork, photos, and other symbols you display activate your future self's mindset and behaviors? Does your environment push you forward or pull you back?

If you are going to really become your future self, you need an environment that reminds you of that future self, not your former self. Goals don't become realities without constant reminders. This is why people write down their goals every single day. They need to remember where they're going, just like an airplane needs to constantly update its trajectory as it gets pushed off course.

> What transformational triggers can you install into your environment?
>
> Where would you put those strategic reminders?

Don't make this too complicated. For instance, you could put a Post-it note on the steering wheel of your car, or on your bathroom mirror, to remind you of something you don't want to forget. Like, "Tell your wife you love her."

Change your computer password to a phrase your future self would use.

Move your television so it is no longer the centerpiece of your home. Better yet, get rid of it and replace it with something better.

Remove all of the social media apps from your phone.

Look at your closet and get rid of anything that your future self wouldn't wear.

You could fill your entire environment with reminders of your highest aspirations and goals. And you should.

Strategic Ignorance

> Your input determines your outlook. Your outlook determines your output, and your output determines your future.
>
> —*Zig Ziglar*

There is a lot of garbage out in the world. Most of the internet is low-level distraction or filth you simply don't need or want to know about.

Most movies are useless.

Most of the news is irrelevant to your situation.

Most people aren't aligned with your future self.

There are seemingly infinite options in the world today. With increased options come increased *choices*. This may seem like a good thing, but for most people it is not. More choices mean more decisions, and as we discussed before, decision fatigue can lead to you getting stuck in negative cycles. A lot of the choices you encounter on a daily basis are endless rabbit holes to nowhere. Instead of keeping the door open to more choices, you need the discernment and confidence to close most doors so you're entirely unaware of them.

Does this add to or take away from my future self?

It's too costly for your mind to be focused on the wrong things, once you become serious about success and change. In the book *The Paradox of Choice*, psychologist Barry Schwartz explains:

- We assume that more choice means better options and greater satisfaction.
- However, choice overload makes you question the decisions you make before you even make them.
- Choice overload leaves you in a perpetual state of FOMO— the fear of missing out—always looking over your shoulder and questioning the decisions you've made.
- This puts you in a constant state of stress, always feeling like you're falling short, always questioning the decisions you've made, always wondering what could have been.

Having options is a good thing. Without options, you can't make choices. However, the best decision-makers in the world purposefully avoid almost all of the options available. Jason Fried, the founder of Basecamp, once said, "I'm pretty oblivious to a lot of things intentionally. I don't want to be influenced that much."

It takes confidence and boldness to say, "I'm going with this decision. This is what I'm committed to. This is what I'm serious about. Consequently, I'm closing the door on everything else right now. I need to focus. I can't be distracted by everyone else's noise and agendas."

If you're serious about achieving goals and intentionally moving forward in your life, you must create an environment that shields you from most of the world.

Strategic ignorance is not about being closed-minded. It's about knowing what you want and knowing that, as a person, you can be easily swayed or derailed. Rather than putting yourself in stupid situations and being forced to rely on willpower due to lack of planning, you simply avoid stupid situations. You even avoid amazing situations that you know are ultimately a distraction to becoming your desired future self.

You create boundaries.

You live your priorities and values and dreams.

Peter Diamandis, one of the world's foremost experts on entrepreneurship and the future of innovation, has said, "I've stopped watching TV news. They couldn't pay me enough money." From his perspective, it's easy to be seduced by the negative and the new.

Diamandis is right. The news is not objective, but a point of view based on selective attention. When you watch the news, you see a story, a subjective view into the world. You can choose to buy into that story, but if you do, your identity and goals will be limited by that view.

Diamandis is strategically ignorant. He's created an environment to shield himself from the distractions and negativity of the news media, while staying informed on the topics he cares about through careful and deliberate research.

Being a successful, creative person requires selective ignorance. Another example is Seth Godin, who purposefully doesn't read the comments on Amazon about his books. He used to do so, but it only left him feeling horrible and questioning himself. So now he has stopped.

Godin is selectively ignorant to what the trolls say, and he's better off as a result. He doesn't need that crap coming into his psyche, confusing his identity and purpose.

Selective ignorance is not the avoidance of learning. It's not the avoidance of getting feedback. It's simply the intelligence of knowing that with certain things and people, the juice will never be worth the squeeze. It's knowing what to avoid.

Without question, Godin gets feedback on his work. But he gets feedback from valued sources that help him create *better work*. He gets feedback that will ultimately move him forward, not feedback intended to destroy him.

Diamandis clearly knows about current events and what is happening in the world. It's essential to the work he does as a futurist and someone trying to create global change. But he gets his information from valued sources. He has designed an environment where only the best information gets to him. He's strategically unaware of everything else.

Selective ignorance is something that must be applied if you're serious about becoming your future self. Your input shapes your identity, biology, and personality. When you change your inputs, all of these change.

Psychologically, if you don't know about something, you probably won't be tempted by it. If you see a plate of cookies on the counter, you're no longer ignorant of them. If you haven't made the decision beforehand, the situation will beat you. If, on the other hand, you simply keep cookies out of your environment, then you won't have to deal with decision fatigue and willpower depletion. You won't have to waste your time thinking about something you already know you don't want.

As it relates to opportunities, it is smart to have systems in place so you don't have to weigh every decision. For example, my assistant and I created rules for opportunities that are presented to her. If they don't meet my criteria, she doesn't present them to me, but instead kindly emails back, telling the sender I can't focus on that right now.

Of course, like the impoverished kids in Charlie Trotter's restaurant, you want exposure to new and higher ways of living. Growth and transformation require becoming conscious of things you're currently unconscious of. Strategic ignorance is about purposefully ignoring or shielding yourself from what you already know is a distraction or an enemy to your future self. It's your filter for ensuring that only the right new things reach you. And this filter will never be perfect, but your systems, as well as your own intuition, get better and faster at disregarding distractions.

In order to create an environment that shields you from the distractions in this world, you need to know what you want. You need to know what you stand for. You need to have rules and systems that stop you from finding yourself in a mire of filth or the daze of endless opportunity.

You need to make one decision that makes a million other decisions either easier, automatic, or irrelevant. This is how you remove decision fatigue. This is how you shield yourself from the onslaught of inputs and agendas seeking your time and attention.

If you're serious about becoming your future self, you'll need to create an environment for strategic ignorance. Think about all of the inputs you're current getting that are sabotaging your future self.

Rather than relying on willpower, how could you become ignorant of these things?

In what areas of your life do you need to apply strategic ignorance?

What simple decisions could you make right now that would eliminate decision fatigue from your life?

What are you currently aware of or overly informed about that you shouldn't be? (Think distractions—for me, sports analysis or the latest updates of various celebrities.)

What distractions or unwanted temptations remain in your world that need to be removed?

Forcing Functions

The ability of the average man could be doubled if it were demanded. If the situation demanded.

—Will Durant

Christina Tosi was born in Ohio and raised in Springfield, Virginia. She graduated college with a degree in math but wasn't sure if that's what she wanted to do. Her mom had taught her to give her heart and soul to whatever she did, so she decided to give her soul to baking and making pastries.

Tosi moved to New York and enrolled in the French Culinary Institute's pastry arts program. She began her culinary career at the fine dining restaurant Bouley, then advanced to the restaurant wd~50 in Manhattan, run by famed chef Wylie Dufresne.

Impressed by Tosi's work ethic, Dufresne recommended David Chang, another famous New York chef, to hire her. Chang didn't hire her to cook or bake but to write his food safety plans and help deal with the administrative requirements of the NYC Department of Health.

Tosi started bringing her homemade pastries into the restaurant and sharing them with the staff. Everyone was blown away, including Chang. There were no desserts on Chang's menu, and he loved Tosi's style. He insisted on several occasions to have one of her desserts served at the restaurant. But she was timid and shy and didn't believe in herself.

Still, she kept making increasingly unique, clever, and delicious desserts for the restaurant staff. Recognizing that she would never do it on her own, one day Chang told her that she had three hours to create something. And whatever she created was going to be served that night.

He was serious. In his own words, "I had to push her off of a cliff. She wouldn't do it herself."

Tosi spent the next three hours creating a brilliant strawberry shortcake. The guests in the restaurant were surprised not only to have a dessert but something truly unique and fabulous.

From that moment forward, Tosi was making pastries at Momofuku Ssäm Bar. A few years later, in 2008, the adjoining store space next to Momofuku Ssäm Bar became available. By this point, Chang and others could see that Tosi had extreme passion, work ethic, and talent.

Chang also saw that she needed a push. Left to her own devices, she wouldn't make the leap to living her dreams. He pushed her "off the cliff" again, challenging her to open her own shop, which she named Milk Bar. The bakery was an immediate success. By 2019, Milk Bar employed 381 people across North America, and Tosi had opened her sixteenth Milk Bar in Boston.

But none of this would have occurred if David Chang hadn't forced her to follow her dream. Chang's giving Tosi three hours to create something was a *forcing function*—he created a situation that forced her to rise up.

A forcing function is any situational element that forces you to take action and produce a result. Forcing functions put you in a situation where the only option is the desired option. You've designed the situation to force you in the direction you want.

That's what happened to Tosi. Deep down, she wanted to make pastries for more people. Chang designed a situation that forced that out of her.

Forcing functions are done to weed out your former self or the distractions so prevalent in life. You're creating a situation that suits your future self, forcing you to show up as that person here and now.

Implementing forcing functions into your life ensures that you're constantly moving in a desired direction, often against your own resistance. Forcing functions require time restraints, which activate Parkinson's law. This law dictates that work expands to fill the time available for its completion. You give yourself a date and you are forced to come up with something by that deadline. Otherwise, nothing gets done.

Embedding forcing functions into your life is done by creating faster feedback loops that are also high-stakes. You want the stakes for performance to be high, otherwise the forcing function isn't powerful enough. For Tosi, her pride was on the line, as was the reputation of the restaurant. She had to perform not only for herself but also for her entire team and for the patrons.

In extreme sports, such as motocross or snowboarding, the inherent danger and immediacy of feedback are powerful forcing functions. If a motocross rider doing backflips over seventy feet doesn't succeed, failure could mean their life. Forcing functions require the highest level of focus and engagement—the goal is psychological flow and high performance.

The situations of your life should be designed and engineered such that you are completely absorbed in what you're doing. You want to be required to produce your absolute best work, because if you don't, the consequences will be costly.

Are you serious about making the changes you want?

Are you willing to put forcing functions into play?

Forcing functions are serious, but they can also be fun. They are actually a way to gamify your life and radically upgrade your motivation to succeed.

One of the most useful and powerful forcing functions is financial investment. By investing money into something, you become more committed. Behavioral economists call this the "sunk cost bias." You commit to what you're invested in. This is usually described as a fallacy, or a mistake in reasoning that makes you throw good money after bad, or waste your time sitting through a show you hate just because you paid for the ticket.

But you can use this tendency to your advantage too. As an example, my friend Draye and I paid more than $800 to sign up for an Ironman Triathlon. I'd never done anything like that before. But we wanted to do something crazy and we knew the only way we'd be serious about it is if we paid to sign up for the race.

So we bit the bullet.

We created a forcing function.

Here's what's amazing, though. Investment is not only the initiation of a decision, it's also the initiation of *enhanced imagination*. Before signing up for the Ironman, I had only passively considered such a thing. Some of my friends had done one, and I was curious, but not serious.

But once we made the investment, *I began thinking about the Ironman a lot*. I began seeing myself, in my mind, engaging in the

Ironman—practice and completion. I was seeing myself as someone who *could* do an Ironman.

That initial investment began shaping my subsequent behaviors. I bought audiobooks about endurance sports and starting listening to them, fueling my input with new ideas. I pulled out my road bike, which I hadn't dusted off in over six years.

I was thinking more and more about the Ironman. My imagination and behavior began shaping my identity. My behavior and other inputs were fueling that new identity. I changed my focus at the gym from weights to cardio.

It all started from a forcing function.

> How can you embed more forcing functions into your life to ensure you become the person you want to be?
>
> What situations could you create that would produce powerful results?

Conclusion

> If we do not create and control our environment, our environment creates and controls us.
>
> —*Marshall Goldsmith*

Environment is among the most powerful and important personality levers. If you're serious about changing yourself and your life, you must change your environment.

You are the product of your culture and context. You're the product of the information and inputs you consume. Everything that comes *in*—the food, information, people, experiences—shapes you. The first step is becoming mindful of your context and how it is having an impact on who you are. The next step is becoming strategic with your environment and situation.

Instead of having your environment and circumstances reflect your identity, you want to design your environment to reflect your future identity. You want your environment to be like a current pulling you forward, not holding you back.

When you change your environment, over time, everything about you will change. You'll begin having new experiences. You'll have new thoughts and emotions. You'll be around new people. You'll be engaging in new behaviors.

Your identity and personality will change.

You can choose the kind of personality you are going to have. It is not something you are stuck with. It is not something you have to have, even if you have never elected anything to the contrary.

—Dr. Wayne Dyer

Embrace Your Future to Change Your Past

> Life is simple. Everything happens for you, not to you.
>
> —*Byron Katie*

On May 19, 2000, Melissa Hull was at her home in Yuma, Arizona. Her husband was away in Phoenix for work for a few days. Melissa was exhausted. Her three-year-old son Devin was very sick and having a hard time sleeping. Melissa had tried to call her husband multiple times to get help with Devin but couldn't reach him.

Around five in the morning, Drew, Melissa's four-year-old son, was ready to wake up. Melissa helped Drew get breakfast, start watching *Thomas & Friends*, and play with crayons. She then went to check on Devin and fell back asleep while lying down with him. She slept from around 5:30 to 7:30 a.m.

When she woke up, she had a horrible feeling in her stomach that told her something was wrong. The house was silent. Drew was usually loud. Melissa spent the next fifteen minutes looking all over the house for Drew. She noticed the sliding glass door was open a few inches and realized he had gone outside.

She looked through the trees on their property and saw Drew's footprints on the dusty paths around their rural home. She followed the prints in the dirt, which led to an irrigation canal near their home. She could see the dirt embankment that had collapsed under Drew's foot and the recent splash on both sides of the canal from his fall.

She started to scream for help. A Border Patrol officer found her soon after and the search began. More than seven hours later, Drew's body was found, eight miles from their home.

During those seven hours, Melissa had been questioned over and over, by the police, by her husband, by other members of her family. *What happened?* they all wanted to know.

Once Drew was found, the questions kept coming, but they sounded different.

How could you let this happen?

Her husband blamed her for the death of their son and left her one month later. Melissa's whole world corroded. Her identity was shocked. She no longer felt like a good mother. She hated herself. She blamed herself for the death of Drew. She felt like she had lost everything—her son, her husband, herself.

She was below rock bottom.

The pain became so bad that she could barely get herself out of bed. She stopped eating and showering. She did what she could to help Devin during the day, but aside from that, she stayed in bed.

At nights after work, Joey, Melissa's husband, would pick up Devin and spend a few hours with him before dropping him back off to sleep at the house with Melissa. During those few lonely hours when she was by herself, Melissa would often drink or take pain pills. Those were some very dark and painful moments when things hurt the most.

Within a few weeks after the accident, life went back to normal for most of the other people in Melissa's life. But she was still fighting a silent battle. Those who cared about her could see that she was struggling, but they didn't know how to help. They ended up avoiding her. Melissa saw clergymen and therapists to try getting help, but nothing was really working.

A few months after Drew's death, Joey took Devin after work and, for the first time, wasn't going to bring him home. Melissa would be home all by herself for the night. She planned to kill herself.

She had saved a bottle of pain pills that had been prescribed to her. She was going to take the pills, drink a lot of alcohol, go to bed, and never wake up. She felt that killing herself was the best thing she could do for Devin, so that he wouldn't have to watch his shell of a mother decay into nothing.

When she went into the kitchen to get the pills and alcohol, she saw a pile of condolence letters on the counter. Over the previous few months, she had gotten many letters in the mail from random strangers who had heard her story in the news. She opened one of the letters, written by a stranger named Theresa.

In the letter, Theresa told Melissa that her six-year-old daughter had been hit by a truck. The accident happened while Theresa had gone inside her house for just a moment. Theresa wrote that she initially blamed herself for her daughter's death, and it took her a long time to stop doing so. She encouraged Melissa not to fault herself for what happened. She told Melissa that she was a great mom, and that this was a tragic accident. She wrote that there could still be joy and happiness in Melissa's life, but she would have to choose it, and choose it again and again every single day.

After reading this letter, Melissa broke down. She grabbed her picture of Drew, held it to her chest, and sobbed for hours. She let all of her bottled-up pain and emotions fully out.

This letter gave her hope. It was the turning point in her life, at the exact moment when she needed it. Theresa was her empathetic witness. She felt heard and seen.

She dumped the pills down the drain.

Instead of the goodbye note she was planning to write to Devin, Melissa wrote an apology letter and a promise to her son. She apologized for falling asleep that morning when Drew died. She apologized that Devin would grow up without a brother. She also apologized for how she had been acting in the months since Drew's death, and how sad she had been.

She made Devin a promise that she would be the best mom she could be for him. She promised him that life would be good. She thanked him for being her reason to try and stay on this planet. She apologized that she might lean on him too much in the future because he was her reason to live. She poured out her heart.

Ten years later, when Devin was thirteen years old and in Melissa's eyes ready to read it, she gave him the letter on Christmas Day. Even though she'd held on to the letter for ten years, she had been true to the promises she wrote. Theresa's letter had changed and saved Melissa's life. She had her ups and downs, but she had hope and purpose to move forward in her life.

Then something else happened.

Less than a year after she gave Devin his letter, Melissa and Joey learned that Joey's assistant had embezzled millions of dollars from their business over the previous decade. While being questioned by the police, Melissa was informed that her husband was having an affair with that same assistant. Melissa didn't believe it.

When she went home one night after being questioned, she told Joey she had been asked the craziest questions about his cheating on her. He didn't make eye contact with her but continued staring at the television set.

"It's true," he told her.

In an instant, something clicked in Melissa's body and the words came out without restraint.

"Oh my God, you were with her when Drew died!"

It was like her whole world collapsed on her at once. The pain was almost too much to bear. She was heartbroken and shattered. She remembered trying to reach her husband that entire morning. Devin had been sick and Joey wasn't answering her phone calls.

It turned out that Joey had been cheating on Melissa for over twelve years. In his own guilt and shame, he had made her life a living hell. He had blamed her for the death of Drew. He had made her feel like less than dirt.

For the next eighteen months, Melissa was tied up dealing with the legalities of the embezzlement and affair. Near the end of the trial, her attorney told her, "Sweetheart, I've been in law for forty years. I don't know anyone with a story like yours. You should write a book about it."

She thought about it and decided to go back through all of her journals, which she had kept throughout her life. While poring over her old journals, she saw a girl who had dealt with a great deal of pain, confusion, and trauma in her life. While reading through the journals, and while journaling and praying at length, she had a paradigm shift.

She began to see her past differently. For most of her life, she had felt like a victim. She had felt like she was cursed by God. But while reading those old journals and reflecting on her experiences, she saw her previous experiences differently. *Rather than curses, she saw compliments.*

"God really trusts you," she thought to herself. "Everything I've gone through is a gigantic compliment from God not only for what I can handle, but for what he wants me to do."

That's a profound and fundamental shift that all people, including you, need to make if you're serious about extreme transformation: Your past isn't happening to you. Your past is happening for you.

Everything in your life has happened *for* you.

You're the beneficiary.

You've gained much.

You've learned much.

And as a result of all the pain and challenges you've gone through, you have a powerful purpose.

It was 2011 when Melissa found out about the affair. In 2014 she started writing her book, which was published in 2016. She's an entirely different person than she was on the morning she woke up in a silent home.

In her own words, "I'm purpose-driven now. I want to dedicate my entire life to helping other people who don't feel heard."

Melissa's purpose is what drives her, not her "personality." Her purpose drives her to do things far outside her comfort zone. Her purpose transforms her and her personality.

Over the years, she's tried to contact Theresa, her empathetic witness. She's made public statements on social media trying to get in contact, but to no avail. Regardless, that letter gave her hope and changed her life. Melissa's entire purpose now is to give hope to those who have lost it. She wants to share her story, to provide people the space to connect with their own inner voice. Her book and her story is her own "letter" to the world, because it was a letter that saved her life.

When I asked Melissa what was most different about her now, she said she is now willing to involve herself in other people's problems. Before all of these transformational experiences, she would just pass by people who were struggling. She was too busy dealing with her own mess to pay attention to other people. But now she's in a place where she has the desire to help others.

When I asked her who her future self was, she said her future self is a powerful force for good. She sees her future self as a bold messenger of hope and healing. She sees herself inspiring and helping many people throughout the world.

When I asked her how her story and past had changed over the years, she said that she has nothing but extreme gratitude. She feels that everything has happened for a reason. Although she's been through hell, she feels it was all worth it because now she has amazing experiences every day.

Recently, she was able to talk to a couple who had lost their daughter in a boating accident. She has such conversations regularly. She gets to be an empathetic witness every single day. And for her, none of this would have been possible without the experiences she's had.

She loves her past.

She loves her life.

She and Joey have forgiven each other and moved on. When Melissa told him she wanted to write a book, detailing everything about her life and marriage, he totally supported it. As a family, they've all made their peace.

Their future is brighter than their past.

Their future continues to change their past.

Now It's Your Turn

You've made it this far. The question is, what are you going to do now? Are you going to be consistent with your former or your future self?

Are you going to activate the four levers of your personality and make radical and desired change?

Are you going to continually expand yourself—imagining and becoming a new future self again and again?

We've covered a lot of ground. We've discussed trauma, story, subconscious, and environment, and how all of these forces can keep you trapped in unhealthy and repetitious cycles. We've also discussed the cultural and pervasive myths of personality, which if you embrace them will lead to a life of mediocrity and "average."

You are now equipped to increase your imagination, motivation, faith, and courage. You are equipped to embrace your future and change your past.

Throughout this book, you've been asked dozens of questions. Go back through those questions and answer them in your journal. Use your journal every single day to imagine, design, strategize, and conspire to create and live your wildest dreams.

Personality isn't permanent, it is a choice.

Your personality can change in dramatic ways. The life of your dreams can eventually become something you take for granted—your new normal. Once you arrive at your wildest and most imaginative future self, take the confidence and faith you gain and do it again, but this time bigger and better.

Life is a classroom. You're here to grow. You're here to live by faith and design. You're here. You're here to choose.

The choice is yours.

Who will you be?

Acknowledgments

Writing this book has been one of the hardest things I've ever done. Its publication date was pushed back twice by my editor, who was incredibly patient with me throughout the yearlong process of putting the pieces together. Thanks to Adrian Zackheim and the entire team at Portfolio for support on this book.

A huge thanks to Kaushik Viswanath, who long before I became a published author or even had a literary agent found my ebook *Slipstream Time Hacking* and saw potential. Thank you for holding this book to a higher standard than I held for myself. Thank you for pushing me to get my thinking right and clear, and for never making me feel inferior or incapable. There were many times throughout the writing of this book that I began to doubt myself. Although you might have as well, especially when it began to look like this might not ever become a book, you never showed any signs of doubt. I'd also like to thank Helen Healey, who also edited the book and supported me getting to the finish line!

To Laurie Liss, thank you for being such a beautiful friend. Thank you for being my agent and seeing potential in me I still don't see for myself. Thank you for holding my work to an increasingly high standard, and for being patient as I mature into a professional. Thank you for all of the phone calls and for the love and support. I am so grateful to have you in my life.

To Tucker Max, you came into this project at a desperate and essential time. Working with you enhanced my writing capabilities in a way I hadn't experienced in several years. You made writing this book fun again, and you showed me how to think differently and better as a writer. I'm blown away and honored that you helped edit this book and mentored me through the process. I've never had more fun writing than when I worked back and forth with you over the three weeks we hashed out the first full draft. Thanks for being a great friend and mentor to me.

To Hal Clifford, for helping me organize the structure and thinking of this book. You helped me accomplish in two weeks what I couldn't do in almost a year without you. The scope and difficulty of the concepts in this book made it very hard to structure. For the first ten or so months, I created probably more than thirty different tables of contents and structures. None of them felt right. The book didn't feel right, and it began to feel like I'd lost touch with what I initially set out to do. But Hal, you brought me back to my core and helped me frame and structure my ideas in a way that allowed me and Tucker to easily flow through the writing process. Thank you again.

To Vanessa O'Brien, Rosalie Clark, Andre Norman, Nate Lambert, Jane Christiansen, and Melissa Hull for letting me use your stories in this book. Without your stories, the ideas in this book would be less powerful and less useful. Thank you for allowing me to ask you questions. Thank you for your vulnerability and trust.

To Dr. Robert Sinclair, who during the writing of this book mentored and guided me through the completion of my PhD in industrial and organizational psychology at Clemson University. Although you likely disagree with much that is written in this book, I will always acknowledge you in all that I do. I almost got kicked out of my PhD program for stupid mistakes I made and for my lack of fitting into the academic structure. You watched me fumble over and over and yet you still allowed me the opportunity to finish. Completing my PhD was one of the most significant accomplishments of my life. I did basically my entire dissertation while writing this book. I could not have done it without your patience, kindness, and nonjudgment toward me and my goals. Thank you, Bob.

To Joe Polish, thank you for being the first domino for so much that has happened in my life since 2017. Thank you for allowing me to speak at the Genius Network Annual Event. Thank you for supporting and helping me in everything I do. Thank you for being a true friend and collaborator. Thank you for being the ultimate "giver" I know. I know that we will be doing lots of E.L.F. projects in the future. I can't wait!

To Dan Sullivan and Babs Smith, thank you for your patience as I wrote this book. You and I have a book project, *Who Not How,* that had to sit on hold while I struggled through this book. In the documentary, *Game Changer*, made about Dan's life, Babs, the cofounder of Strategic Coach, said about him, "He has a different way of looking at time. And it helps people to be on their own time, and not on the time the world tries to impose on them. 'This is your window.' 'You have to act now.' He's like, 'No you don't.'" I have experienced this myself. Dan, thank you for teaching me about 10X Thinking and 100X Collaborations. Thank you for creating a 25 Year Collaboration with me. It's going to be explosive.

To Richie Norton, Richard Paul Evans, Wayne Beck, Jason Korman, Draye Redfern, Chad Willardson, Whitney Bishop, Aubrey Luddington, Eric McKibbin, Alan and Linda Burns, Ross and Krissi Allred, and everyone else who is a core relationship in my personal and professional life: *Thank you for your love and support!* It means the world to me!

To Kay and Janae Anderson, thank you for allowing me to be married to your daughter. Thanks for taking a chance on a "White"! Thanks for all the love and support you've given me in creating my dreams. Your love and support, both emotionally and financially, have been essential to my succeeding the way I have. Thank you for being such incredible people in my life. I love every interaction I get to have with you.

To my own parents, Philip Hardy and Susan Knight, thank you for being my parents. Thank you for bringing me into this world. Thank you for loving me unconditionally, and for always supporting me in my goals and dreams. Thank you for being my best friends and my biggest cheerleaders. Thank you for all you've taught me and continue to teach me. To Trevor and Jacob, thank you for being my brothers. Thank you for the loving bond we have together. Thank you for your empathy and patience with me as your older brother, especially during the hardest time in our lives. I wasn't who I needed to be for you guys. But looking back now, I think we all have a better understanding and empathy toward our past. I love you both forever.

To Lauren, thank you for being my wife. Thank you for dealing with countless nights with me either staying up late writing or traveling. Thank you for creating and maintaining order in our lives. Thank you for being a solid rock in my life. Thank you for your faith, love, generosity, thoughtfulness, and patience for me. My love for you increases every day. I hope that I can become the man you deserve and see me as. To Kaleb, Jordan, Logan, Zorah, and Phoebe, thanks for being my kids. Thanks for being a huge inspiration and motivation in my life. Thanks for your patience with my imperfections as a father. I love you all very much and love being your dad. You challenge me to become better every day.

To my Heavenly Parents, thank you for my life. Thank you for everything that is. Thank you for this experience and for the reality of learning and change. I know that I am literally your child, and that I have the capacity to one day become like you. Thank you for always being with me. Thank you for guiding me. Thank you for everything you've blessed me with in my life. Thank you for transforming my past and guiding my future.

Notes

Epigraph

xi   *"stops in interesting places"*: Paul Gardner quoted in "'A Painting Is Never Finished—It Simply Stops in Interesting Places'—Paul Gardner," British International School Hanoi, October 10, 2014, nordangliaeducation.com/en/our-schools/vietnam/hanoi/bis/article/2014/10/10/a-painting-is-never-finished-it-simply-stops-in-interesting-places--paul-gardner.

Introduction: A Personality Test Almost Ruined My Life

1   *seek fun and are the life of the party:* Taylor Hartman, *The People Code: It's All About Your Innate Motive* (New York: Simon & Schuster, 2007).

2   *Facebook had to ban personality quizzes:* Jacob Kastrenakes, "Facebook Bans Personality Quizzes After Cambridge Analytica Scandal," *The Verge*, April 25, 2019, theverge.com/2019/4/25/18516608/facebook-personality-quiz-ban-cambridge-analytica.

3   *hope to improve for the better:* Nathan W. Hudson and R. Chris Fraley, "Volitional Personality Trait Change: Can People Choose to Change Their Personality Traits?," *Journal of Personality and Social Psychology* 109, no. 3 (2015): 490.

3   *caused by prior conditions or events:* Carl Hoefer, "Causal Determinism," in *Stanford Encyclopedia of Philosophy,* ed. Edward N. Zalta, plato.stanford.edu/entries/determinism-causal/; Kadri Vihvelin, "Arguments for Incompatibilism," in ibid., plato.stanford.edu/entries/incompatibilism-arguments/.

4   *especially newly unearthed data:* Jordi Quoidbach, Daniel T. Gilbert, and Timothy D. Wilson, "The End of History Illusion," *Science* 339, no. 6115 (2013): 96–98.

4   *Frankl called the last of human freedoms:* Viktor E. Frankl, *Man's Search for Meaning* (New York: Simon & Schuster, 1985).

5   *the less constrained you'll be by your circumstances:* David R. Hawkins, *Power vs. Force: The Hidden Determinants of Human Behavior* (Carlsbad, CA: Hay House, 2013).

5   *"we truly are, far more than our abilities":* J. K. Rowling, *Harry Potter and the Chamber of Secrets* (London: Bloomsbury, 2015; originally published 1998).

7   *Outsiders may view the hyper-successful:* Carol S. Dweck, *Mindset: The New Psychology of Success* (New York: Random House Digital, 2008).

8   *"What's past is prologue":* William Shakespeare, *The Tempest*, act 2, scene 1.

9   *live out the end of his life on Mars:* Ashlee Vance, *Elon Musk: Tesla, SpaceX, and the Quest for a Fantastic Future* (New York: HarperCollins, 2015).

10 *"Steel can be any shape you want if you are skilled enough":* Robert M. Pirsig, *Zen and the Art of Motorcycle Maintenance: An Inquiry into Values* (New York: Random House, 1999; originally published 1974).

Chapter 1: The Myths of Personality

17 *"Human beings are works in progress":* Daniel Gilbert, "The Psychology of Your Future Self," TED Talk, March 2014, ted.com/talks/dan_gilbert_you_are_always _changing.

22 *woman to climb K2:* "Hero Mountain Climber Visits British High Commission," Diplomatic News Agency (DNA), August 15, 2017, dnanews.com.pk/hero -mountain-climber-visits-british-high-commission/.

22 *fastest time by any woman:* "Mountaineering," *Guinness Book of World Records 2017* (pdf), vobonline.com/wp-content/uploads/2016/12/GWR17.pdf.

24 *everyone's personality is going to change:* Gilbert, "The Psychology of Your Future Self."

26 *"Such a man would be in the lunatic asylum":* Carl Jung, *Psychological Types* (New York: Routledge, 2016; originally published 1921).

26 *In the 2018 book* The Personality Brokers: Merve Emre, *The Personality Brokers: The Strange History of Myers-Briggs and the Birth of Personality Testing* (New York: Doubleday, 2018).

28 *"illusion of expertise about psychology":* Emma Goldberg, "Personality Tests Are the Astrology of the Office," *The New York Times,* September 17, 2019, nytimes.com /2019/09/17/style/personality-tests-office.html.

28 *"the merit of a proposed theory":* Adam Grant, "Goodbye to MBTI, the Fad That Won't Die," *Psychology Today,* September 19, 2013, psychologytoday.com/us/blog /give-and-take/201309/goodbye-mbti-the-fad-won-t-die.

28 *Myers-Briggs should not be taken seriously:* Grant, "Say Goodbye to MBTI, the Fad That Won't Die"; Michael Moffa, "A Critique of The Myers Briggs Type Indicator (MBTI)—Part I: One Expert's Review," Recruiter, April 1, 2011, recruiter.com/i /critique-of-the-myers-briggs-type-indicator-critique/.

29 *"the dumber they make you":* Paul Graham, "Keep Your Identity Small," paulgraham .com, February 2009, paulgraham.com/identity.html.

29 *greatly limiting their capacity to change:* William R. Miller and Stephen Rollnick, *Motivational Interviewing: Preparing People to Change Addictive Behavior* (New York: Guilford Press, 2002).

29 *seeing all of the times the label isn't true:* Ellen J. Langer, *The Power of Mindful Learning* (Boston: Lifelong Books/A Merloyd Lawrence Book, 2016).

30 *"personality than I would trust my horoscope":* Kate Rogers quoted in Theresa Fisher, "I Have Personality Test Anxiety," *Woolly,* woollymag.com/feelings/i-have -personality-test-anxiety.html.

30 *for the position or culture:* Goldberg, "Personality Tests Are the Astrology of the Office."

30 *scientifically backed theory of personality:* Lewis R. Goldberg, "An Alternative 'De-

scription of Personality': The Big-Five Factor Structure," *Journal of Personality and Social Psychology* 59, no. 6 (1990): 1216.

31 *demands of a social role and one's personality profile:* Daniel Heller, Wei Qi Elaine Perunovic, and Daniel Reichman, "The Future of Person–Situation Integration in the Interface Between Traits and Goals: A Bottom-up Framework," *Journal of Research in Personality* 43, no. 2 (2009): 171–78.

31 *tangible predictor of personality:* Daniel J. Ozer and Veronica Benet-Martinez, "Personality and the Prediction of Consequential Outcomes," *Annual Review of Psychology* 57 (2006): 401–21.

32 *people reported being satisfied with themselves:* Nathan W. Hudson and Brent W. Roberts, "Goals to Change Personality Traits: Concurrent Links Between Personality Traits, Daily Behavior, and Goals to Change Oneself," *Journal of Research in Personality* 53 (2014): 68–83.

32 *goal-setting and sustained personal effort:* Nathan W. Hudson and R. Chris Fraley, "Volitional Personality Trait Change: Can People Choose to Change Their Personality Traits?," *Journal of Personality and Social Psychology* 109, no. 3 (2015): 490.

32 *leading meaningful and satisfying lives:* Christopher J. Soto, "Is Happiness Good for Your Personality? Concurrent and Prospective Relations of the Big Five with Subjective Well-Being," *Journal of Personality* 83, no. 1 (2015): 45–55; Jule Specht, Boris Egloff, and Stefan C. Schmukle, "Examining Mechanisms of Personality Maturation: The Impact of Life Satisfaction on the Development of the Big Five Personality Traits," *Social Psychological and Personality Science* 4, no. 2 (2013): 181–89.

33 **Les Misérables by Victor Hugo:** Victor Hugo, *Les Misérables* (Paris: Librairie internationale A. Lacroix, Verboeckhoven, et Cie, 1862).

34 *flummoxed by what they found:* Mathew A. Harris, Caroline E. Brett, Wendy Johnson, and Ian J. Deary, "Personality Stability from Age 14 to Age 77 Years," *Psychology and Aging* 31, no. 8 (2016): 862.

35 **Harvard psychologist Dr. Daniel Gilbert:** Jordi Quoidbach, Daniel T. Gilbert, and Timothy D. Wilson, "The End of History Illusion," *Science* 339, no. 6115 (2013): 96–98.

38 *"goal for which you might strive":* Dallin H. Oaks, "Where Will This Lead?," Church of Jesus Christ of Latter-day Saints, churchofjesuschrist.org/study/general-conference /2019/04/35oaks.

38 *"understanding long-term decision-making":* Hal E. Hershfield, "The Self over Time," *Current Opinion in Psychology* 26 (2019): 72–75.

40 *"past deserves a second chance":* Malcolm Gladwell, *Revisionist History* podcast, revisionisthistory.com/seasons.

40 *antecedent conditions or events:* Carl Hoefer, "Causal Determinism," in *Stanford Encyclopedia of Philosophy,* ed. Edward N. Zalta, plato.stanford.edu/entries /determinism-causal/; Kadri Vihvelin, "Arguments for Incompatibilism," in ibid., plato.stanford.edu/entries/incompatibilism-arguments/.

42 *the worst films of that year:* BoxOfficeMojo.com on film version of *I Hope They Serve Beer in Hell,* boxofficemojo.com/release/rl140215809/.

42 *one of his greatest disappointments:* Tom Bilyeu, "How to Totally Reinvent Yourself | Tucker Max on Impact Theory," YouTube, January 9, 2018, youtube.com/watch?v= RJaczGjkS3w.

43   *"set a public end to this"*: Michael Ellsberg, "Tucker Max Gives Up the Game: What Happens When a Bestselling Player Stops Playing?," *Forbes*, January 18, 2012, forbes.com/sites/michaelellsberg/2012/01/18/tucker-max-gives-up-the-game /#e700de1758dd.

45   *"future goals so affect our memories"*: Brent D. Slife, *Time and Psychological Explanation* (Albany: SUNY Press, 1993).

46   *"I met a man who had no feet"*: Saadi Shirazi, *The Gulistan, or, Rose Garden of Sa'Di* (London: George Allen & Unwin, 1964).

49   *"but in having new eyes"*: Marcel Proust, *La Prisonnière* (Paris: Le Livre de Poche, 2011; originally published 1923).

49   *toward chosen goals or values:* Todd B. Kashdan and Jonathan Rottenberg, "Psychological Flexibility as a Fundamental Aspect of Health," *Clinical Psychology Review* 30, no. 7 (2010): 865–78.

52   *"what you do for a living is much less important"*: Cal Newport, *So Good They Can't Ignore You: Why Skills Trump Passion in the Quest for Work You Love* (New York: Grand Central Publishing, 2012).

52   *"feel yourself into action"*: Jerome S. Bruner, *On Knowing: Essays for the Left Hand,* 2nd ed. (Cambridge, MA: Belknap Press of Harvard University Press, 1979).

57   *"happiness is worth devoting yourself to"*: Clayton Christensen, *How Will You Measure Your Life?* (New York: Harper Business, 2012).

59   *"class and give them a choice not to"*: Taylor Lorenz, "Teens Are Protesting In-Class Presentations," *Atlantic,* September 12, 2018, theatlantic.com/education /archive/2018/09/teens-think-they-shouldnt-have-to-speak-in-front-of-the-class /570061/.

61   *"true to the self I wanted to become"*: Adam Grant, "USU 2017 Commencement Speech—Dr. Adam Grant," YouTube, May 12, 2017, youtube.com/watch?v= YJeLTHsbSug.

Chapter 2: The Truth of Personality

65   *"Without having a goal it's difficult to score"*: Paul Arden, *It's Not How Good You Are, It's How Good You Want to Be* (New York: Phaidon, 2003).

74   *"unexamined life is not worth living"*: Plato, *Euthyphro, Apology of Socrates, and Crito,* ed. John Burnet (Oxford: Clarendon Press, 1977).

78   *better restaurant than Trotter's:* Patrick Cole, "David Bouley, Charlie Trotter to Cook for Disabled Kids," *Bloomberg,* May 30, 2012, bloomberg.com/news/articles /2012-05-31/david-bouley-charlie-trotter-to-cook-for-disabled-kids.

79   *"your personal experiences aren't broad enough"*: David Brooks, "The Man Wishes He Were Here." *The New York Times,* August 29, 2019, nytimes.com/2019/08/29 /opinion/jim-mattis-trump.html.

85   *"outcome of an intentional attitude"*: Colin Wilson, *New Pathways in Psychology: Maslow and the Post-Freudian Revolution* (London: Victor Gallancz, 1972).

87   *"imagination embraces the entire world"*: Albert Einstein quoted in Alice Calaprice, *The Expanded Quotable Einstein* (Princeton, NJ: Princeton University Press, 2000).

87   *engage in deliberate practice:* Thomas Suddendorf, Melissa Brinums, and Kana Imuta, "Shaping One's Future Self—The Development of Deliberate Practice," in *Seeing the Future: Theoretical Perspectives on Future-Oriented Mental Time Travel,*

ed. Kourken Michaelian, Stanley B. Klein, and Karl K. Szpunar, 343–66 (New York: Oxford University Press, 2016).

88 *"somebody to keep on chasing"*: Matthew McConaughey, "Matthew McConaughey Winning Best Actor," YouTube, March 11, 2014, youtube.com/watch?v=wD2cVhC-63I.

90 *"achieve everything else I want in my life"*: Hal Elrod, *The Miracle Equation: The Two Decisions That Move Your Biggest Goals from Possible, to Probable, to Inevitable* (New York: Harmony Books, 2019).

92 *"completely unknowable future"*: Peter Thiel with Blake Masters, *Zero to One: Notes on Startups, or How to Build the Future* (New York: Broadway Business, 2014).

92 *According to* expectancy theory, *one of the:* Wendelien Van Eerde and Henk Thierry, "Vroom's Expectancy Models and Work-Related Criteria: A Meta-analysis," *Journal of Applied Psychology* 81, no. 5 (1996): 575.

92 *You cannot have motivation without a goal:* C. R. Snyder, Kevin L. Rand, and David R. Sigmon, "Hope Theory: A Member of the Positive Psychology Family," in *Handbook of Positive Psychology*, ed. C. R. Snyder and Shane Lopez, 257–76 (New York: Oxford University Press, 2002).

93 *"The result is proof of a commitment"*: Jim Dethmer, Diana Chapman, and Kaley Klemp, *The 15 Commitments of Conscious Leadership: A New Paradigm for Sustainable Success* (Conscious Leadership Group, 2015).

94 *In a podcast, Lewis Howes:* John Assaraf. Retrieved in December 2019 at lewishowes .com/podcast/john-assaraf/.

97 *your willpower is all dried up:* Roy F. Baumeister and John Tierney, *Willpower: Rediscovering the Greatest Human Strength* (New York: Penguin, 2012).

100 *how you become self-actualized:* Abraham H. Maslow, "Peak Experiences as Acute Identity Experiences," *American Journal of Psychoanalysis* 21, no. 2 (1961): 254–62.

100 *"effect upon the experimenter"*: Abraham H. Maslow, *Religions, Values, and Peak-Experiences* (Columbus: Ohio State University Press, 1964).

101 *"If there is no choice, there is no uncertainty"*: Ellen J. Langer, *The Power of Mindful Learning* (Boston: Lifelong Books/A Merloyd Lawrence Book, 2016; originally published 1997).

101 predict *the outcomes of our behavior:* Daphna Shohamy, "Learning from Experience: How Our Brains Remember the Past and Shape Our Future," YouTube, April 7, 2016, youtube.com/watch?v=vCPtpXaH5Zw.

102 *in actuality the foundation of all fears:* R. N. Carlton, "Fear of the Unknown: One Fear to Rule Them All?," *Journal of Anxiety Disorders* 41 (2016): 5–21.

102 *incorrectly predict what will happen:* G. Elliott Wimmer, Erin Kendall Braun, Nathaniel D. Daw, and Daphna Shohamy, "Episodic Memory Encoding Interferes with Reward Learning and Decreases Striatal Prediction Errors," *Journal of Neuroscience* 34, no. 45 (2014): 14901–12.

103 *"honing of skills through deliberate practice"*: Suddendorf, Brinums, and Imuta, "Shaping One's Future Self."

105 *gratitude has been found to help:* Philip C. Watkins, Kathrane Woodward, Tamara Stone, and Russell L. Kolts, "Gratitude and Happiness: Development of a Measure of Gratitude, and Relationships with Subjective Well-Being," *Social Behavior and Personality: An International Journal* 31, no. 5 (2003): 431–51.

105 *affects emotional well-being:* Laura Redwine et al., "A Pilot Randomized Study of a Gratitude Journaling Intervention on HRV and Inflammatory Biomarkers in Stage B Heart Failure Patients," *Psychosomatic Medicine* 78, no. 6 (2016): 667.

107 *following the Heisman Trophy award:* Joe Burrow, interview with ESPN, January 6, 2020, youtube.com/watch?v=O-CJBHcAUOM.

Chapter 3: Transform Your Trauma

111 *"every new encounter or event is contaminated by the past":* Bessel van der Kolk, *The Body Keeps the Score: Brain, Mind, and Body in the Healing of Trauma* (New York: Penguin, 2015).

113 *a universal force that stops people:* Steven Pressfield, *The War of Art: Break Through the Blocks and Win Your Inner Creative Battles* (New York: Black Irish Entertainment LLC, 2002).

114 *mental shutdown when facing mathematics:* Jennifer Ruef, "Think You're Bad at Math? You May Suffer from 'Math Trauma,'" *The Conversation*, November 1, 2018, theconversation.com/think-youre-bad-at-math-you-may-suffer-from-math -trauma-104209.

115 *often score zero on imagination:* Van der Kolk, *The Body Keeps the Score.*

115 *Stanford psychologist Carol Dweck:* Carol S. Dweck, *Mindset: The New Psychology of Success* (New York: Random House Digital, 2008).

116 *a fixed mindset is a "premature cognitive commitment":* Benzion Chanowitz and Ellen J. Langer, "Premature Cognitive Commitment," *Journal of Personality and Social Psychology* 41, no. 6 (1981): 1051.

116 *exaggerated fear of failure:* Dweck, *Mindset.*

117 *"obstacles but by a clear path to a lesser goal":* Robert Brault, *Round Up the Usual Subjects: Thoughts on Just About Everything* (CreateSpace, 2014).

118 *"true self at all but the loss of it":* Gabor Maté, *In the Realm of Hungry Ghosts: Close Encounters with Addiction* (Berkeley, CA: North Atlantic Books, 2011).

119 *Singer's book* The Untethered Soul: Michael Singer, *The Untethered Soul: The Journey Beyond Yourself* (Oakland, CA: New Harbinger Publications, 2007).

121 *"the day I hung up my sneakers":* Kobe Bryant, *The Mamba Mentality: How I Play* (New York: MCD, 2018).

123 *As the author Dr. Joe Dispenza states:* Joe Dispenza, "How to Unlock the Full Potential of Your Mind | Dr. Joe Dispenza on Impact Theory," YouTube, June 12, 2018, youtube.com/watch?v=La9oLLoI5Rc.

124 *"absence of an empathetic witness":* Peter A. Levine and Ann Frederick, *Waking the Tiger: Healing Trauma* (Berkeley, CA: North Atlantic Books, 1997).

124 *survivors don't report the abuse:* National Sexual Violence Resource Center, "Statistics About Sexual Violence," nsvrc.org/sites/default/files/publications_nsvrc _factsheet_media-packet_statistics-about-sexual-violence_0.pdf.

125 *"feel inferior without your consent":* Quoted in *Reader's Digest* 37, no. 221 (September 1940): 84.

127 *twenty-six-year-old client, Joan Frances Casey:* Joan Frances Casey and Lynn I. Wilson, *The Flock: The Autobiography of a Multiple Personality* (New York: Ballantine, 1992).

130 *TV personality Lisa Ling:* Tim Ferriss, "Lisa Ling—Exploring Subcultures, Learning

to Feel, and Changing Perception (#388)," *Tim Ferriss Blog,* tim.blog/2019/09/26
/lisa-ling/.

133 *"serious trouble and you will be right":* Henry Eyring, "Try, Try, Try," Church of Jesus Christ of Latter-day Saints, churchofjesuschrist.org/study/general-conference
/2018/10/try-try-try.

133 *mutual trust and understanding occur:* David L. Cooperrider and Diana Kaplin
Whitney, *Appreciative Inquiry: A Positive Revolution in Change* (San Francisco, CA:
Berrett-Koehler, 2005).

Chapter 4: Shift Your Story

139 *"Contained in those memories are not just the events":* Gordon Livingston, *Too
Soon Old, Too Late Smart: Thirty True Things You Need to Know Now* (Boston: Lifelong Books, 2009).

140 *"What does a man do for an encore":* Buzz Aldrin and Ken Abraham, *Magnificent Desolation: The Long Journey Home from the Moon* (New York: Three Rivers Press, 2010).

141 *"But let's go for the next goal":* "The Jump: Rachel Nichols Interviews Giannis Antetokounmpo," YouTube, July 22, 2019, youtube.com/watch?v=e3yh284Fkok.

141 *"future bigger than your past":* Dan Sullivan and Catherine Nomura, *The Laws of
Lifetime Growth: Always Make Your Future Bigger Than Your Past* (Oakland, CA:
Berrett-Koehler, 2016).

144 *"Meaning connects things":* Roy F. Baumeister, *Meanings of Life* (New York: Guilford
Press, 1991).

144 *create meaning from our experiences:* Crystal L. Park, "Making Sense of the Meaning Literature: An Integrative Review of Meaning Making and Its Effects on Adjust-
ment to Stressful Life Events," *Psychological Bulletin* 136, no. 2 (2010): 257.

146 *"We see the world, not as it is, but as we are":* Stephen R. Covey, *The 7 Habits of
Highly Effective People: Powerful Lessons in Personal Change* (New York: Simon &
Schuster, 2004; originally published 1989).

149 *manage something you're not aware of:* Alicia A. Grandey, "Emotional Regulation
in the Workplace: A New Way to Conceptualize Emotional Labor," *Journal of Oc-
cupational Health Psychology* 5, no. 1 (2000): 95.

153 *unity and purpose to our lives:* Dan P. McAdams and Kate C. McLean, "Narrative
Identity," *Current Directions in Psychological Science* 22, no. 3 (2013): 233–38.

154 *Dan Sullivan calls "the gap and the gain":* Dan Sullivan, *The Gap and the Gain,*
Strategic Coach, now.strategiccoach.com/the-gap-and-the-gain-ebook.

157 *winning bestseller* **Growing Up:** Russell Baker, *Growing Up* (New York: Rosetta-
Books, 2011; originally published 1982).

157 *"color our past either happy or sad":* Livingston, *Too Soon Old, Too Late Smart.*

163 *"totally false with each retrieval":* D. J. Bridge and K. A. Paller, "Neural Correlates
of Reactivation and Retrieval-Induced Distortion," *Journal of Neuroscience* 32, no.
35 (2012): 12144–51.

165 *even if imperceptibly:* Kamal Ravikant, *Love Yourself Like Your Life Depends on It*
(CreateSpace, 2012).

168 *"hold to your principles":* Clayton Christensen, *How Will You Measure Your Life?*
(New York: Harper Business, 2012).

171 *"Make your vision of where you want to be a reality"*: Paul Arden, *It's Not How Good You Are, It's How Good You Want to Be* (New York: Phaidon, 2003).

174 *"There's a million things I haven't done"*: Lin-Manuel Miranda, Alex Lacamoire, and Ron Chernow, *Hamilton: An American Musical* (Atlantic Recording Corporation, 2015).

Chapter 5: Enhance Your Subconscious

177 *"characteristics that drive us to behave as we do"*: John E. Sarno, *Healing Back Pain: The Mind-Body Connection* (New York: Warner Books, 1991).

184 *his book:* The Body Keeps the Score: Bessel van der Kolk, *The Body Keeps the Score: Brain, Mind, and Body in the Healing of Trauma* (New York: Penguin, 2015).

184 *"turning experience into biology"*: Steven Cole quoted in David Dobbs, "The Social Life of Genes," *Pacific Standard*, September 3, 2013, psmag.com/social-justice/the -social-life-of-genes-64616.

185 *our brain and body is emotions:* Candace B. Pert, *Molecules of Emotion: Why You Feel the Way You Feel* (New York: Simon & Schuster, 1997).

185 *subconscious loop you've played out:* Joe Dispenza, *Breaking the Habit of Being Yourself: How to Lose Your Mind and Create a New One* (Carlsbad, CA: Hay House, 2012).

186 *"familiar zone where we feel secure"*: Gay Hendricks, *The Big Leap: Conquer Your Hidden Fear and Take Life to the Next Level* (New York: HarperCollins, 2009).

188 *the only way to alter your subconscious:* Candice Pert, "Your Body Is Your Subconscious Mind" (audio CD) (Louisville, CO: Sounds True, 2004).

188 *easier for us to live with physical pain:* Sarno, *Healing Back Pain.*

189 *"unconscious mind: which is the body"*: Steven Ray Ozanich, *The Great Pain Deception: Faulty Medical Advice Is Making Us Worse,* 1st ed. (Warren, OH: Silver Cord Records, 2011).

189 *either cope with or avoid them:* Van der Kolk, *The Body Keeps the Score.*

190 *"The best of all medicines are rest and fasting"*: Benjamin Franklin in Tryon Edwards (ed.), *A Dictionary of Thoughts* (Detroit, MI: F. B. Dickerson Co., 1907), 339.

190 *nicotine, alcohol, caffeine, and other drugs:* "Dr. Cinque's Facts about Fasting." Retrieved in December 2019 at drcinque.com/facts.html.

190 *confidence while reducing your anxiety:* J. L. Chan, J. E. Mietus, Mietus, P. M. Raciti, A. L. Goldberger, and C. S. Mantzoros, "Short-term Fasting-induced Autonomic Activation and Changes in Catecholamine Levels Are Not Mediated by Changes in Leptin Levels in Healthy Humans," *Clinical Endocrinology* 66, no. 1 (2006): 49–57.

190 *increases your number of brain cells:* B. Martin, M. P. Mattson, and S. Maudsley, "Caloric Restriction and Intermittent Fasting: Two Potential Diets for Successful Brain Aging," *Ageing Research Reviews* 5, no. 3 (2006): 332–53.

190 *increase your longevity and lifespan:* B. D. Horne, C. Bartholomew, J. L. Anderson, H. T. May, K. U. Knowlton, T. L. Bair, and J. B. Muhlestein, "Intermittent Fasting Lifestyle and Human Longevity in Cardiac Catheterization Populations," *Circulation* 140, no. suppl_1 (2019): A11123.

190 *age-related declines in cognitive and motor abilities:* R. Singh, S. Manchanda, T. Kaur, S. Kumar, D. Lakhanpal, S. S. Lakhman, and G. Kaur, "Middle Age Onset

Short-Term Intermittent Fasting Dietary Restriction Prevents Brain Function Impairments in Male Wistar Rats," *Biogerontology* 16, no. 6 (2015): 775–88.

190 *cognitive stressors that bring about:* J. B. Johnson, W. Summer, R. G. Cutler, B. Martin, D-H Hyun, V. D. Dixit, M. Pearson, M. Nassar, R. Tellejohan, S. Maudsley, O. Carlson, S. John, D. R. Laub, and M.R. Mattson, "Alternate Day Calorie Restriction Improves Clinical Findings and Reduces Markers of Oxidative Stress and Inflammation in Overweight Adults with Moderate Asthma," *Free Radical Biology and Medicine* 42, no. 5 (2007): 665–74.

190 *improve the overall quality of your sleep:* A. Michalsen, F. Schlegel, A. Rodenbeck, R. Lüdtke, G. Huether, H. Teschler, and G. J. Dobos, "Effects of Short-Term Modified Fasting on Sleep Patterns and Daytime Vigilance in Non-Obese Subjects: Results of a Pilot Study," *Annals of Nutrition and Metabolism* 47, no. 5 (2003): 194–200.

190 *ability to comprehend information:* Á. Fontán-Lozano, J. L. Sáez-Cassanelli, M. C. Inda, M. de los Santos-Arteaga, S. A. Sierra-Domínguez, G. López-Lluch, G., and Á. M. Carrión, "Caloric Restriction Increases Learning Consolidation and Facilitates Synaptic Plasticity Through Mechanisms Dependent on NR2B Subunits of the NMDA Receptor," *Journal of Neuroscience* 27, no. 38 (2007): 10185–95.

190 *empty stomach helps you think:* T. L. Horvath and S. Diano, "The Floating Blueprint of Hypothalamic Feeding Circuits," *Nature Reviews Neuroscience* 5, no. 8 (2004): 662–67.

190 *better focus on their creative work:* Gladwell, Malcom, *The Tim Ferriss Show Transcripts*: Malcolm Gladwell (#168). Retrieved December 2019 at tim.blog/2018/06/01/the-tim-ferriss-show-transcripts-malcolm-gladwell/.

192 *"actively to assist in your quest":* Rabbi Daniel Lapin, *Thou Shall Prosper: Ten Commandments for Making Money* (Hoboken, NJ: John Wiley & Sons, 2009).

192 *charitable giving was linked with feelings of happiness:* W. T. Harbaugh, U. Mayr, and D. R. Burghart, "Neural Responses to Taxation and Voluntary Giving Reveal Motives for Charitable Donations," *Science* 316 (5831): 1622–25.

192 *providing charitable donations are linked to happiness:* E. W. Dunn, L. B. Aknin, and M. I. Norton, "Spending Money on Others Promotes Happiness," *Science* 319, no. 5870 (2008): 1687–88.

192 *happiness is related to successful outcomes:* Shawn Achor, *The Happiness Advantage: The Seven Principles That Fuel Success and Performance at Work* (London: Virgin, 2011).

193 *"had paid tithing on the year before":* Wendy Watson Nelson, "Becoming the Person You Were Born to Be," Church of Jesus Christ of Latter-day Saints, January 10, 2016, churchofjesuschrist.org/broadcasts/article/worldwide-devotionals/2016/01/becoming-the-person-you-were-born-to-be?lang=eng.

194 *"The ocean doesn't care":* Mark Victor Hansen and Robert G. Allen, *The One Minute Millionaire: The Enlightened Way to Wealth* (New York: Three Rivers Press, 2009).

Chapter 6: Redesign Your Environment

197 *"the fate of the cells was controlled":* Bruce H. Lipton, *The Biology of Belief: Unleashing the Power of Consciousness, Matter and Miracles* (Carlsbad, CA: Hay House, 2005).

197 *the home to a group of eight men:* Ellen J. Langer, *Counterclockwise: Mindful Health and the Power of Possibility* (New York: Ballantine, 2009).

200 *"his time plays many parts":* William Shakespeare, *As You Like It,* act 2, scene 7.

201 *"the power of the situation":* Lee Ross and Richard E. Nisbett, *The Person and the Situation: Perspectives of Social Psychology* (London: Pinter & Martin, 2011; originally published 1991).

202 *lacks recognition that in different situations:* Brent D. Slife and Bradford J. Wiggins, "Taking Relationship Seriously in Psychotherapy: Radical Relationality," *Journal of Contemporary Psychotherapy* 39, no. 1 (2009): 17.

202 *From a relational worldview:* Brent D. Slife, "Taking Practice Seriously: Toward a Relational Ontology," *Journal of Theoretical and Philosophical Psychology* 24, no. 2 (2004): 157; Brent D. Slife and Frank C. Richardson, "Problematic Ontological Underpinnings of Positive Psychology: A Strong Relational Alternative," *Theory and Psychology* 18, no. 5 (2008): 699–723.

203 *peer group powerfully influences your behavior:* Gina Tomé et al., "How Can Peer Group Influence the Behavior of Adolescents: Explanatory Model," *Global Journal of Health Science* 4, no. 2 (2012): 26.

204 *cultures view personality differently:* Rachid Laajaj et al., "Challenges to Capture the Big Five Personality Traits in Non-WEIRD Populations," *Science Advances* 5, no. 7 (2019): eaaw5226.

205 *"responses across the two tests were pretty consistent":* Christopher Soto, "The Famous Big 5 Personality Test Might Not Reveal the True You," NPR, July 10, 2019, npr .org/sections/goatsandsoda/2019/07/10/740214086/the-famous-big-5-personality -test-might-not-reveal-the-true-you.

206 *"what I have done I can do again":* James Whistler quoted in Sterling W. Sill, "Great Experiences," Church of Jesus Christ of Latter-day Saints, churchofjesuschrist.org /study/general-conference/1971/04/great-experiences.

207 *"a lot of empty yesterdays":* Meredith Willson, *The Music Man* (1957).

210 *"your output determines your future":* Zig Ziglar, *Goals* (New York: Simon & Schuster Audio, 1995).

211 *psychologist Barry Schwartz explains:* Barry Schwartz, *The Paradox of Choice: Why More Is Less* (New York: Ecco, 2004).

211 *"oblivious to a lot of things intentionally":* Tim Ferriss, "Jason Fried—How to Live Life on Your Own Terms (#329)," *Tim Ferriss Blog,* tim.blog/2018/07/23/jason -fried/.

212 *"I've stopped watching TV news":* Peter Diamandis, "What the News Media Won't Tell You About Global Violence," diamandis.com/blog/what-the-news-media-wont -tell-you-about-global-violence.

215 *"If the situation demanded":* Will Durant and Ariel Durant, *The Lessons of History* (New York: Simon & Schuster, 2012; originally published 1968).

216 *sixteenth Milk Bar in Boston:* Christina Tosi, *Chef's Table,* Netflix, www.netflix.com /title/80007945.

217 *designed the situation to force:* Herman J. Damveld, Gijs C. Beerens, Marinus M. Van Paassen, and Max Mulder, "Design of Forcing Functions for the Identification of Human Control Behavior," *Journal of Guidance, Control, and Dynamics* 33, no. 4 (2010): 1064–81.

217 *goal is psychological flow:* Steven Kotler, *The Rise of Superman: Decoding the Science of Ultimate Human Performance* (New York: Houghton Mifflin Harcourt, 2014).

219 *"our environment creates and controls us":* Marshall Goldsmith and Mark Reiter, *Triggers: Creating Behavior That Lasts—Becoming the Person You Want to Be* (New York: Crown Business, 2015).

220 *"never elected anything to the contrary":* Wayne W. Dyer, *Your Erroneous Zones* (audio) (New York: Funk & Wagnalls, 1976).

Conclusion: Embrace Your Future to Change Your Past

221 *"Everything happens for you, not to you":* Byron Katie and Stephen Mitchell, *Loving What Is: How Four Questions Can Change Your Life* (New York: Random House, 2008).

Index